The Acts of the Apostles

Part Two

The Acts of the Apostles
Part Two

Acts 15:36–28:31

Dennis Hamm

with Little Rock Scripture Study staff

Little Rock
Scripture Study

LITURGICAL PRESS
Collegeville, Minnesota

www.littlerockscripture.org

Nihil obstat for the commentary text by Dennis Hamm: Robert C. Harren, *Censor deputatus.*
Imprimatur for the commentary text by Dennis Hamm: ✠ John F. Kinney, Bishop of St. Cloud, Minnesota, August 30, 2005.

Cover design by John Vineyard. Interior art by Ned Bustard. Maps on pages 10, 21, 29, and 61 created by Ann Blattner. Map on page 65 created by Clifford M. Yeary with Ann Blattner. Photos and illustrations on pages 17, 34, 50, 57, and 67 courtesy of Getty Images; page 30 courtesy of Wikimedia Commons; page 31 courtesy of Ronald D. Witherup, PSS.

 This symbol indicates material that was created by Little Rock Scripture Study to supplement the biblical text and commentary. Some of these inserts first appeared in the *Little Rock Catholic Study Bible*; others were created specifically for this book by Catherine Upchurch.

1   2   3   4   5   6   7   8   9

Library of Congress Cataloging-in-Publication Data

Names: Hamm, M. Dennis, author. | Little Rock Scripture Study Staff, author.
Title: The Acts of the Apostles / Dennis Hamm with Little Rock Scripture Study staff.
Description: Collegeville, MN : Liturgical Press, [2021] | Contents: Part one (Acts 1:1-15:35) — Part two (Acts 15:36-28:31). | Summary: "A Bible study exploring the early church as the apostles of Jesus become evangelists and pastors, as communities of believers expand to include Gentiles, and as local challenges test the staying power of the young church. Commentary, study and reflection questions, prayers, and access to online lectures are included"— Provided by publisher.
Identifiers: LCCN 2020056014 (print) | LCCN 2020056015 (ebook) | ISBN 9780814665244 (paperback) | ISBN 9780814665510 (paperback) | ISBN 9780814665497 (v. 1 : epub) | ISBN 9780814665497 (v. 1 : mobi) | ISBN 9780814665497 (v. 1 : pdf) | ISBN 9780814665756 (v. 2 : epub) | ISBN 9780814665756 (v. 2 : mobi) | ISBN 9780814665756 (v. 2 : pdf)
Subjects: LCSH: Bible. Acts—Study and teaching. | Bible. Acts—Commentaries.
Classification: LCC BS2626 .H284 2021 (print) | LCC BS2626 (ebook) | DDC 226.6/077—dc23
LC record available at https://lccn.loc.gov/2020056014
LC ebook record available at https://lccn.loc.gov/2020056015

TABLE OF CONTENTS

Wrap-Up Lectures and Discussion Tips for Facilitators are available for each lesson at no charge. Find them online at LittleRockScripture.org/Lectures/ActsPartTwo.

Welcome

The Bible is at the heart of what it means to be a Christian. It is the Spirit-inspired word of God for us. It reveals to us the God who created, redeemed, and guides us still. It speaks to us personally and as a church. It forms the basis of our public liturgical life and our private prayer lives. It urges us to live worthily and justly, to love tenderly and wholeheartedly, and to be a part of building God's kingdom here on earth.

Though it was written a long time ago, in the context of a very different culture, the Bible is no relic of the past. Catholic biblical scholarship is among the best in the world, and in our time and place, we have unprecedented access to it. By making use of solid scholarship, we can discover much about the ancient culture and religious practices that shaped those who wrote the various books of the Bible. With these insights, and by praying with the words of Scripture, we allow the words and images to shape us as disciples. By sharing our journey of faithful listening to God's word with others, we have the opportunity to be stretched in our understanding and to form communities of love and learning. Ultimately, studying and praying with God's word deepens our relationship with Christ.

The Acts of the Apostles, Part Two
Acts 15:36–28:31

The resource you hold in your hands is divided into four lessons. Each lesson involves personal prayer and study using this book and the experience of group prayer, discussion, and wrap-up lecture.

If you are using this resource in the context of a small group, we suggest that you meet four times, discussing one lesson per meeting. Allow about 90 minutes for the small group gathering. Small groups function best with eight to twelve people to ensure good group dynamics and to allow all to participate as they wish.

Some groups choose to have an initial gathering before their regular sessions begin. This allows an opportunity to meet one another, pass out books, and, if desired, view the optional intro lecture for this study available on the "Resources" page of the Little Rock Scripture Study website (www.littlerockscripture.org). Please note that there is only one intro lecture for two-part studies.

Every Bible study group is a little bit different. Some of our groups like to break each lesson up into two weeks of study so they are reading less each week and have more time to discuss the questions together at their weekly gatherings. If your group wishes to do this, simply agree how much of each lesson will be read each week, and only answer the questions that correspond to the material you read. Wrap-up lectures can then be viewed at the end of every other meeting rather than at the end of every meeting. Of course, this will mean that your study will last longer, and your group will meet more times.

WHAT MATERIALS WILL YOU USE?

The materials in this book include:

- The text of the Acts of the Apostles, chapters 15:36–28:31, using the New American Bible, Revised Edition as the translation.
- Commentary by Dennis Hamm (which has also been published separately as part of the New Collegeville Bible Commentary series).
- Occasional inserts 🔥 highlighting elements of the chapters of Acts being studied. Some of these appear also in the *Little Rock Catholic Study Bible* while others are supplied by staff writers.
- Questions for study, reflection, and discussion at the end of each lesson.
- Opening and closing prayers for each lesson, as well as other prayer forms available in the closing pages of the book.

In addition, there are wrap-up lectures available for each lesson. Your group may choose to purchase a DVD containing these lectures or make use of the video lectures available online at no charge. The link to these free lectures is: LittleRockScripture.org/Lectures/ActsPartTwo. Of course, if your group has access to qualified speakers, you may choose to have live presentations.

Each person will need a current translation of the Bible. We recommend the *Little Rock Catholic Study Bible*, which makes use of the New American Bible, Revised Edition. Other translations, such as the New Jerusalem Bible or the New Revised Standard Version: Catholic Edition, would also work well.

HOW WILL YOU USE THESE MATERIALS?

Prepare in advance

Using Lesson One as an example:

- Begin with a simple prayer like the one found on page 11.

- Read the assigned material for Lesson One (pages 12–22) so that you are prepared for the weekly small group session.
- Answer the questions, Exploring Lesson One, found at the end of the assigned reading, pages 23–25.
- Use the Closing Prayer on page 26 when you complete your study. This prayer may be used again when you meet with the group.

Meet with your small group

- After introductions and greetings, allow time for prayer (about 5 minutes) as you begin the group session. You may use the prayer on page 11 (also used by individuals in their preparation) or a prayer of your choosing.
- Spend about 45–50 minutes discussing the responses to the questions that were prepared in advance. You may also develop your discussion further by responding to questions and interests that arise during the discussion and faith-sharing itself.
- Close the discussion and faith-sharing with prayer, about 5–10 minutes. You may use the Closing Prayer at the end of each lesson or one of your choosing at the end of the book. It is important to allow people to pray for personal and community needs and to give thanks for how God is moving in your lives.
- Listen to or view the wrap-up lecture associated with each lesson (15–20 minutes). You may watch the lecture online, use a DVD, or provide a live lecture by a qualified local speaker. View the lecture together at the end of the session or, if your group runs out of time, you may invite group members to watch the lecture on their own time after the discussion.

A note to individuals

- If you are using this resource for individual study, simply move at your own pace. Take as much time as you need to read, study, and pray with the material.
- If you would like to share this experience with others, consider inviting a friend or family member to join you for your next study. Even a small group of two or three provides an opportunity for fruitful dialog and faith-sharing!

The World of Paul

Black Sea

Mediterranean Sea

Aegean Sea

MACEDONIA
ACHAIA
ITALIA
MALTA
CRETE
RHODES
LYCIA
GALATIA
ASIA
CILICIA
CYPRUS
SYRIA

Rome
Byzantium
Philippi
Thessalonica
Beroea
Athens
Corinth
Troas
Ephesus
Colossae
Antioch
Iconium
Lystra
Perga
Myra
Paphos
Tarsus
Antioch
Sidon
Damascus
Tyre
Ptolemais
Caesarea
Antipatris
Joppa
Jerusalem
Alexandria

200 km
0

100 miles
0

10

The Acts of the Apostles

Part Two

LESSON ONE

Introduction and Acts 15:36–18:28

Begin your personal study and group discussion with a simple and sincere prayer such as:

Prayer

God of the Universe, we marvel at those who first carried the good news to the far reaches of the earth. Allow these sacred readings to encourage us to carry the gospel into the world where we live.

Read the Introduction on page 12 and the Bible text of Acts 15:36–18:28 found in the outside columns of pages 13–22, highlighting what stands out to you.

Read the accompanying commentary to add to your understanding.

Respond to the questions on pages 23–25, Exploring Lesson One.

The Closing Prayer on page 26 is for your personal use and may be used at the end of group discussion.

INTRODUCTION

The Acts of the Apostles, Part Two, covers the second half of the book of Acts (15:36–28:31). As a "refresh" for those already in the midst of studying Acts, and as a brief introduction for those joining the process midstream, the following background information may be helpful.

The Acts of the Apostles tells the story of the earliest days of the church. The events described in Acts occurred immediately following the death and resurrection of Jesus and continued into the first generation of believers. These events took place prior to the writing of the Gospels. It is fair to say, then, that as the apostles began to evangelize and tell the story of Jesus, they honed their ability to shape the stories we find in the Gospels. In other words, the apostles focused keenly on the words and deeds of Jesus that would open the hearts of their listeners.

The author of the Third Gospel, the evangelist we know as Luke, is also the author of the Acts of the Apostles. Both books are addressed to a "Theophilus" (Luke 1:1-4; Acts 1:1). The first book, the Gospel of Luke, covers the life, death, resurrection, and ascension of Jesus. The second book, the Acts of the Apostles, takes up the story with a resurrection appearance and the ascension of Jesus, and then follows some of Jesus' followers as they begin to share the good news beyond the reaches of Judea and into the vastness of the Roman Empire.

While it remains a mystery why the other three evangelists did not also write an account of some of the apostles, it is clear that Luke felt a sequel to his Gospel was needed. Why? By the time Luke was writing (A.D. 80–90), the church was increasingly composed of Gentiles (non-Jews). Perhaps these Christian communities that were a mixture of Jewish and Gentile backgrounds needed an understanding of how the church came to include both. Perhaps they would see that their experience was the flowering of God's promise that Israel would be "a light to the nations" (Isa 49:6).

Luke also wrote Acts to demonstrate that the life of Christians, individually and communally, is always to some extent patterned after the life of Jesus. Thus Stephen's death parallels Jesus' death, the travels and trials of Paul mirror the travels and trials of Jesus, etc. Even early on, believers needed to discover that Jesus was relevant in their own time, not just in the years he walked the earth.

Perhaps Luke also had an apologetic reason for writing the Acts of the Apostles. Apologetics is the discipline of demonstrating the worthiness and truth of a system of belief or body of practices. In the vastness of the Roman Empire, imperial power grew, and emperors themselves became the object of worship. In such an environment, Christianity probably seemed to emerge as a threat. By demonstrating Christianity's honorable roots in Judaism, which was tolerated in the empire, Luke paves a way for the acceptance of Christianity. This is one of the reasons readers will find references to the ways that Christ fulfilled Israel's expectations throughout the book of Acts.

About one-third of the content of Acts is taken up with speeches. Some of these speeches occur as sermons to invite listeners to belief, to conversion, and to a new way of life. Other speeches are testimonies by the followers of Jesus when they are taken into custody or are standing trial. These speeches are not simply the reporting of facts; instead, they are intended to convince and convert, to sway and support, to deliberate and defend.

The early success of the gospel among Gentiles, and the formal acceptance of Gentiles as a result of the Council of Jerusalem, occurred in Part One of our study of the Acts of the Apostles. The apostle Peter played a large role in those early chapters, along with Barnabas, James, and a few others. The later chapters of Acts, which are the subject of this study, largely feature Paul and several of his companions as they make their way across the Roman Empire and into its heart, Rome.

As we accompany Paul on these journeys, we will discover a tireless missionary and an apostle who is on fire with the good news of Jesus Christ. Let us begin!

THE MISSION OF PAUL TO THE ENDS OF THE EARTH

Acts 15:36–28:31

The travels described in Acts 16–20 cover two more distinct journeys, the second and third missionary journeys of Paul (and companions). And each journey has a distinct geographical center of gravity: as the first addressed communities in southern Galatia, the second concentrates on major cities in Macedonia and Achaia, and the third centers in, and radiates from, the great Ephesus.

Like the first journey described in chapters 13–14, the second and third also begin and return to Syrian Antioch and include one major speech by Paul—the only address to a Gentile audience (in Athens, 17:22-31) and the farewell address at Miletus to the Ephesian elders (20:18-35). Yet because these two journeys are separated by what is only a brief return to Syrian Antioch (18:22), it may be helpful (and even more faithful to Luke's narrative) to think of the activities recounted in these five chapters as the Aegean mission. Together, these travels form a whole, moving from what Paul himself refers to as "the beginning of the gospel" at Philippi (Phil 4:15) to Paul's "last will and testament" addressed to the Ephesian elders at

Miletus (Acts 20:17-38). The remainder of the book (Acts 21–28) is a distinct segment devoted to journeys related to Paul's Jewish and Roman imprisonment and "trials" (really hearings) in Jerusalem and Caesarea Maritima, and finally house arrest in Rome.

15:36-41 Paul and Barnabas separate

Luke's delicate treatment of the interplay between the human intentions and divine will continues to unfold dramatically. What will eventually become Paul's greatest missionary expansion begins simply with the intention of revisiting and strengthening the churches he had founded in the first mission (Acts 13–14). That God can work with the results of human frailty is implied in Luke's notice that Paul and Barnabas had a "disagreement" (whose depth is suggested by the Greek word here, *paroxysmos*, v. 38, from which the English "paroxysm" derives) about whether Mark, who had deserted the previous mission at Pamphylia, should be allowed to accompany them. Thus the breakup

V: The Mission of Paul to the Ends of the Earth

Paul and Barnabas Separate

[36]After some time, Paul said to Barnabas, "Come, let us make a return visit to see how the brothers are getting on in all the cities where we proclaimed the word of the Lord." [37]Barnabas wanted to take with them also John, who was called Mark, [38]but Paul insisted that they should not take with them someone who had deserted them at Pamphylia and who had not continued with them in their work. [39]So sharp was their disagreement that they separated. Barnabas took Mark and sailed to Cyprus. [40]But Paul chose Silas and departed after being commended by the brothers to the grace of the Lord. [41]He traveled through Syria and Cilicia bringing strength to the churches.

continue

CHAPTER 16

Paul in Lycaonia: Timothy

¹He reached [also] Derbe and Lystra where there was a disciple named Timothy, the son of a Jewish woman who was a believer, but his father was a Greek. ²The brothers in Lystra and Iconium spoke highly of him, ³and Paul wanted him to come along with him. On account of the Jews of that region, Paul had him circumcised, for they all knew that his father was a Greek. ⁴As they traveled from city to city, they handed on to the people for observance the decisions reached by the apostles and presbyters in Jerusalem. ⁵Day after day the churches grew stronger in faith and increased in number.

Through Asia Minor

⁶They traveled through the Phrygian and Galatian territory because they had been prevented by the holy Spirit from preaching the message in the province of Asia. ⁷When they came to Mysia, they tried to go on into Bithynia, but the Spirit of Jesus did not allow them, ⁸so they crossed through Mysia and came down to Troas. ⁹During [the] night Paul had a vision. A Macedonian stood before him and implored him with these words, "Come over to Macedonia and help us." ¹⁰When he had seen the vision, we sought passage to Macedonia at once, concluding that God had called us to proclaim the good news to them.

Into Europe

¹¹We set sail from Troas, making a straight run for Samothrace, and on the next day to Neapolis, ¹²and from there to Philippi, a leading city in that district of Macedonia and a Roman colony. We spent some time in that city. ¹³On the sabbath we went outside the city gate along the river where we thought there would be a place of prayer. We sat and spoke with the women who had gathered there. ¹⁴One of them, a woman named Lydia, a dealer in purple cloth, from the city of Thyatira, a worshiper of God, listened, and the Lord

continue

of the first team leads to the formation of a powerful new team—Paul and Silas. First introduced in verses 22-32 as a leader in the Jerusalem community and a prophet, Silas is usually taken to be the same person as the Silvanus mentioned in the New Testament epistles.

16:1-5 Timothy joins Paul and Silas

This brief passage shows Paul's nuanced approach to Jewish/Gentile relations in the Christian mission. Even as he continues to promulgate the apostolic decree of the Council of Jerusalem (15:23-29), which frees Gentile converts from having to become Jews, he can still insist that Timothy undergo adult circumcision. Apparently Timothy was raised Jewish by his mother (named Eunice, we learn in 2 Timothy 1:5) but had never been circumcised (prevented by his Greek father?). That Paul convinced him to get circumcised, even though he was now a Christian, suggests that Paul still considered mission to Jews important enough to take this surprising step to make Timothy more acceptable to his fellow Jews.

 Timothy was one of Paul's most beloved companions (1 Cor 4:17; Phil 2:19-22). Paul frequently relied on him as a messenger to his congregations (Acts 19:22; 1 Thess 3:2), and according to Acts, he joined Paul on his second and third missionary journeys (16:3; 20:4). Two New Testament letters (1 and 2 Timothy) are addressed to Timothy, offering instruction and encouragement as Timothy pastors his own flock in Ephesus. Although these letters are attributed to Paul, scholars are unsure whether Paul himself penned them.

16:6-10 The call to Macedonia

The movement of this team of three into fresh mission territory presents again the delicate interface of the divine and human in their decision-making. As they move westward, they are prevented from moving south by the holy Spirit and from moving north by "the Spirit of Jesus." When Paul receives a dream vision of a Macedonian calling for help, that call still requires ratification by human decision (v. 10).

A note on the "we" passages

The introduction of the first person plural ("we") in verse 10 signals the first of the famous four "we" sections in Acts (16:10-17; 20:5-15; 21:1-18; 27:1–28:16). To account for this phenomenon, commentators have noted that the first person plural was sometimes used in ancient travel narratives as a literary device to evoke immediacy. However, this does not appear to be the case with Acts, a work of history. The abruptness of the shifts from third-person narrative to first-person (and back again) is more easily accounted for as deriving from the actual involvement of the author (or his sources). Moreover, ancient historians were eager to indicate their presence at the events they described when they had grounds to make such a claim. We have no evidence of their making such claims groundlessly.

16:11-15 The conversion of Lydia and her household

Seeking a Jewish house of prayer, Paul, Silas, Timothy (and Luke, if we understand "we" historically) encounter a group of women gathered by the riverside. With marvelous economy of words, Luke describes one Lydia. She is a businesswoman, a dealer in the luxury item of purple cloth, a God fearer, and wealthy enough to be mistress of a household. Such is her openness and response to Paul's sharing of the word that Luke describes it in language reminiscent of the conversion of the Emmaus pair in Luke 24:31-32: "The Lord opened her heart." Conversion and baptism lead immediately to generous hospitality. Since the missioners later return to "Lydia's house" (v. 40) after their release from prison, she may well have emerged as the leader of the first house church of Philippi (and thus the first in what will later be known as Europe).

opened her heart to pay attention to what Paul was saying. [15]After she and her household had been baptized, she offered us an invitation, "If you consider me a believer in the Lord, come and stay at my home," and she prevailed on us.

Imprisonment at Philippi

[16]As we were going to the place of prayer, we met a slave girl with an oracular spirit, who used to bring a large profit to her owners through her fortune-telling. [17]She began to follow Paul and us, shouting, "These people are slaves of the Most High God, who proclaim to you a way of salvation." [18]She did this for many days. Paul became annoyed, turned, and said to the spirit, "I command you in the name of Jesus Christ to come out of her." Then it came out at that moment.

[19]When her owners saw that their hope of profit was gone, they seized Paul and Silas and dragged them to the public square before the local authorities. [20]They brought them before the magistrates and said, "These people are Jews and are disturbing our city [21]and are advocating customs that are not lawful for us Romans to adopt or practice." [22]The crowd joined in the attack on them, and the magistrates had them stripped and ordered them to be beaten with rods. [23]After inflicting many blows on them, they threw them into prison and instructed the jailer to guard them securely. [24]When he received these instructions, he put them in the innermost cell and secured their feet to a stake.

Deliverance from Prison

[25]About midnight, while Paul and Silas were praying and singing hymns to God as the prisoners listened, [26]there was suddenly such a severe earthquake that the foundations of the jail shook; all the doors flew open, and the chains of all were pulled loose. [27]When the jailer woke up and saw the prison doors wide open, he drew [his] sword and was about to kill himself, thinking that the prisoners had escaped. [28]But Paul shouted out in a loud voice, "Do no harm to yourself; we are all

continue

here." [29]He asked for a light and rushed in and, trembling with fear, he fell down before Paul and Silas. [30]Then he brought them out and said, "Sirs, what must I do to be saved?" [31]And they said, "Believe in the Lord Jesus and you and your household will be saved." [32]So they spoke the word of the Lord to him and to everyone in his house. [33]He took them in at that hour of the night and bathed their wounds; then he and all his family were baptized at once. [34]He brought them up into his house and provided a meal and with his household rejoiced at having come to faith in God.

[35]But when it was day, the magistrates sent the lictors with the order, "Release those men." [36]The jailer reported the[se] words to Paul, "The magistrates have sent orders that you be released. Now, then, come out and go in peace." [37]But Paul said to them, "They have beaten us publicly, even though we are Roman citizens and have not been tried, and have thrown us into prison. And now, are they going to release us secretly? By no means. Let them come themselves and lead us out." [38]The lictors reported these words to the magistrates, and they became alarmed when they heard that they were Roman citizens. [39]So they came and placated them, and led them out and asked that they leave the city. [40]When they had come out of the prison, they went to Lydia's house where they saw and encouraged the brothers, and then they left.

CHAPTER 17

Paul in Thessalonica

[1]When they took the road through Amphipolis and Apollonia, they reached Thessalonica, where there was a synagogue of the Jews. [2]Following his usual custom, Paul joined them, and for three sabbaths he entered into discussions with them from the scriptures, [3]expounding and demonstrating that the Messiah had to suffer and rise from the dead, and that "This is the Messiah, Jesus, whom I proclaim to you." [4]Some of them were convinced and joined Paul and Silas; so, too, a great number of Greeks who were worshipers,

continue

16:16-40 Further adventures in Philippi: deliverance, imprisonment, and further deliverance

On his way to the house of prayer, Paul encounters some unsolicited and annoying advertising. A slave girl with a mantic spirit goes around shouting what is in fact the truth: "These people are slaves of the Most High God, who proclaim to you a way of salvation" (v. 17). Though true enough in a Christian context, the ambiguous language would have been heard by pagans as announcing Paul and Silas as promoting a new cure in the name of the god that they promote as the top god of the pagan pantheon. When Paul puts a stop to this with a command in the name of Jesus and the woman is delivered of the oracular spirit, her exploiters, distressed by the loss of business, bring the missioners before the Roman magistrates. The charge: illegal (anti-imperial) proselytizing.

The twosome are stripped, beaten, and imprisoned. During the night an earthquake opens the jail doors and unchains the prisoners. When the jailer finds the missioners freed but still present, he responds to these portents by falling on his knees and asking, "What must I do to be saved?" And they say, "Believe in the Lord Jesus and you and your household will be saved." As in the case of Lydia, openness leads to conversion of a household, hospitality, and baptism.

When the Roman authorities realize their mistake and try to dismiss Paul and friends discreetly, Paul confronts the police. He and his men are Roman citizens, and he insists that their beating and imprisonment without trial are a miscarriage of justice that ought to be reversed, not secretly but officially. This elicits a sheepish apology from the magistrates, who come to apologize and to ask them to leave town. This they do, but not without stopping at Lydia's place to encourage the budding Philippian community.

17:1-15 From Thessalonica to Beroea, with mixed reviews

Although Luke treats Paul's mission in Thessalonica (some hundred miles west of Philippi) as a brief, three-week encounter, the community he founded there was significant enough to receive the earliest letter we have from the Apostle's hand, 1 Thessalonians.

The events here are described in language that resonates with the Third Gospel. When Luke notes that Paul joined the local synagogue community according to "his usual custom," he could be referring to Paul's usual missionary strategy. He could as well mean that Paul attended synagogue as his Jewish practice, much as Jesus attended the Nazareth synagogue "according to his custom" (Luke 4:16). His teaching in that house of prayer and study is summarized in words that reflect the message of Jesus to the disciples on Easter Sunday ("The Messiah had to suffer and rise from the dead," v. 3; see Luke 24:26, 46-47). And when those in the Jewish community who find Paul's message a threat drag to the magistrates some of the small Christian community growing in Jason's place, their accusations echo those leveled against Jesus: "They all act in opposition to the decrees of Caesar and claim instead that there is another king, Jesus" (v. 7; see Luke 23:2).

Some sixty miles to the southwest, Paul and Silas find a much more receptive synagogue in Beroea, where people engage the missioners in biblical study, not just on the Sabbath but "daily" (v. 11). But the zealous Thessalonian

and not a few of the prominent women. [5]But the Jews became jealous and recruited some worthless men loitering in the public square, formed a mob, and set the city in turmoil. They marched on the house of Jason, intending to bring them before the people's assembly. [6]When they could not find them, they dragged Jason and some of the brothers before the city magistrates, shouting, "These people who have been creating a disturbance all over the world have now come here, [7]and Jason has welcomed them. They all act in opposition to the decrees of Caesar and claim instead that there is another king, Jesus." [8]They stirred up the crowd and the city magistrates who, upon hearing these charges, [9]took a surety payment from Jason and the others before releasing them.

Paul in Beroea

[10]The brothers immediately sent Paul and Silas to Beroea during the night. Upon arrival they went to the synagogue of the Jews. [11]These Jews were more fair-minded than those in Thessalonica, for they received the word with all willingness and examined the scriptures daily to determine whether these things were so. [12]Many of them became believers, as did not a few of the influential Greek women and men. [13]But when the Jews of Thessalonica learned that the word of God had now been proclaimed by Paul in Beroea also, they came there too to cause a commotion and stir up the crowds. [14]So the brothers at once sent Paul on his way to the seacoast, while Silas and Timothy remained behind. [15]After Paul's escorts had taken him to Athens, they came away with instructions for Silas and Timothy to join him as soon as possible.

Acropolis of Athens, viewed from the Areopagus

continue

Paul in Athens

[16]While Paul was waiting for them in Athens, he grew exasperated at the sight of the city full of idols. [17]So he debated in the synagogue with the Jews and with the worshipers, and daily in the public square with whoever happened to be there. [18]Even some of the Epicurean and Stoic philosophers engaged him in discussion. Some asked, "What is this scavenger trying to say?" Others said, "He sounds like a promoter of foreign deities," because he was preaching about 'Jesus' and 'Resurrection.' [19]They took him and led him to the Areopagus and said, "May we learn what this new teaching is that you speak of? [20]For you bring some strange notions to our ears; we should like to know what these things mean." [21]Now all the Athenians as well as the foreigners residing there used their time for nothing else but telling or hearing something new.

Paul's Speech at the Areopagus

[22]Then Paul stood up at the Areopagus and said:

"You Athenians, I see that in every respect you are very religious. [23]For as I walked around looking carefully at your shrines, I even discovered an altar inscribed, 'To an Unknown God.' What therefore you unknowingly worship, I proclaim to you. [24]The God who made the world and all that is in it, the Lord of heaven and earth, does not dwell in sanctuaries made by human hands, [25]nor is he served by human hands because he needs anything. Rather it is he who gives to everyone life and breath and everything. [26]He made from one the whole human race to dwell on the entire surface of the earth, and he fixed the ordered seasons and the boundaries of their regions, [27]so that people might seek God, even perhaps grope for him and find him, though indeed he is not far from any one of us. [28]For 'In him we live and move and have our being,' as even some of your poets have said, 'For we too are his offspring.' [29]Since therefore we are the offspring of God, we

continue

adversaries soon arrive to stir up the crowds against them, much as the pre-Christian Paul (Saul) traveled distances to block the spread of what he had determined was a dangerous Jewish heresy, "the Way" (Acts 9:2).

17:16-34 Paul in Athens

In this episode Luke presents Paul giving the only fully developed speech to a Gentile audience. He describes that audience with care when he highlights the Stoics and Epicureans in verse 18 (both named only here in the New Testament). The mere mention of the names evokes stereotyped philosophical positions regarding humanity, nature, and the gods. Stoics perceived reality as a unified, organic cosmos in which the divinity inhered pantheistically as a kind of "law." Humanity was part of that cosmos and found happiness by harmonizing with that essentially benevolent law of the cosmos.

Epicureans, on the other hand, had a more mechanistic notion of the world, in which the divine was conceived in a "deistic" way at best (the divinity causing the cosmos but remaining uninvolved with it). Epicureans expected mere dissolution after death and, meanwhile, sought happiness by prudently doing what was most sensibly pleasant. It makes sense, then, for Luke to describe the crowd reactions as divided. On the one hand, there were those who heckled Paul, dismissing him as a "seed-pecker" ("scavenger"; v. 18), a reaction that fits the Epicureans, who would have found Paul's teaching radically incompatible with their own. On the other hand, there were those who were initially confused (thinking Paul to be speaking of new gods, *Iēsous* and *Anastasis* ["Resurrection," misheard as the name of the divine consort of *Iēsous*?]) yet remained open to the preacher and wanted to hear more. And this reaction fits the Stoics, who would have found some tantalizing convergences with their worldview and lifestyle and would have been drawn to further inquiry.

The notion that the deity is not captured in sanctuaries and does not need human worship (see 7:48) would have been congenial to Stoics and Epicureans alike. But against Stoic pantheism, Paul asserts the biblical notion of a transcendent creator who *made* everything and, moreover, sustains everything. Paul reminds them of the common origin of the human family ("made from one"—compatible with the biblical account of origin from Adam and also the fresh beginning with Noah). Echoing his brief proclamation to the Lycaonians at Lystra, Paul remodels LXX Isaiah 42:5 and calls them to contemplate the earth with its seasons as a habitat for humanity and a revelation of the Creator's care.

Where he might have cited Scripture for a synagogue audience, here Paul enlists instead an ancient Stoic poet from his region, Aratus ("for we too are his offspring"), and he also quotes a sixth-century B.C. author, Epimenides of Knossos: "In him we live and move and have our being." Thus Luke appropriates Hellenistic language to assert against Stoic pantheism what we might call a biblical pan*en*theism. Against the Stoic notion of endless cycles of cosmic rebirth and death, he announces the biblical doomsday. Against the coldness of Epicurean "deism," he asserts the biblical notion of God's intimate involvement with creatures. If Luke has said in verse 24 that human handicraft cannot *house* God, in verse 29 he argues that human skill and wit cannot *image* the divinity. The unexpressed element of the argument is the biblical idea that the only adequate image of the living God is living human beings, who are images of the King of the universe insofar as they are stewards of the earth.

If Jesus is going to be the ultimate judge of the human family, it would follow that the criteria are what we have heard him teach in the Third Gospel, especially in the Sermon on the Plain (Luke 6:20-49).

Commentators have noted that Paul is portrayed using this philosophical "natural theology" approach just this once in Acts. And in his first letter to the Corinthians, he makes a point of not coming to them with the wisdom of philosophers but simply with the "foolishness" of a crucified Messiah. Was the approach of Paul in Athens simply a failed strategy,

---

ought not to think that the divinity is like an image fashioned from gold, silver, or stone by human art and imagination. [30]God has overlooked the times of ignorance, but now he demands that all people everywhere repent [31]because he has established a day on which he will 'judge the world with justice' through a man he has appointed, and he has provided confirmation for all by raising him from the dead."

[32]When they heard about resurrection of the dead, some began to scoff, but others said, "We should like to hear you on this some other time." [33]And so Paul left them. [34]But some did join him, and became believers. Among them were Dionysius, a member of the Court of the Areopagus, a woman named Damaris, and others with them.

CHAPTER 18

Paul in Corinth

[1]After this he left Athens and went to Corinth. [2]There he met a Jew named Aquila, a native of Pontus, who had recently come from Italy with his wife Priscilla because Claudius had ordered all the Jews to leave Rome. He went to visit them [3]and, because he practiced the same trade, stayed with them and worked, for they were tentmakers by trade. [4]Every sabbath, he entered into discussions in the synagogue, attempting to convince both Jews and Greeks.

continue

---

never to be repeated? It would seem, rather, that the church has seen in this episode a model of how Jerusalem can speak to Athens. Thomas Aquinas, for example, used the philosophical categories of a rediscovered Aristotle to speak to his European culture. And theology has always been an effort to recast the givens of revelation in the language of one's own time and place. One can even see in this brief masterpiece hints of the basis for the interreligious dialogue that challenges us today.

⁵When Silas and Timothy came down from Macedonia, Paul began to occupy himself totally with preaching the word, testifying to the Jews that the Messiah was Jesus. ⁶When they opposed him and reviled him, he shook out his garments and said to them, "Your blood be on your heads! I am clear of responsibility. From now on I will go to the Gentiles." ⁷So he left there and went to a house belonging to a man named Titus Justus, a worshiper of God; his house was next to a synagogue. ⁸Crispus, the synagogue official, came to believe in the Lord along with his entire household, and many of the Corinthians who heard believed and were baptized. ⁹One night in a vision the Lord said to Paul, "Do not be afraid. Go on speaking, and do not be silent, ¹⁰for I am with you. No one will attack and harm you, for I have many people in this city." ¹¹He settled there for a year and a half and taught the word of God among them.

Accusations before Gallio

¹²But when Gallio was proconsul of Achaia, the Jews rose up together against Paul and brought him to the tribunal, ¹³saying, "This man is inducing people to worship God contrary to the law." ¹⁴When Paul was about to reply, Gallio spoke to the Jews, "If it were a matter of some crime or malicious fraud, I should with reason hear the complaint of you Jews; ¹⁵but since it is a question of arguments over doctrine and titles and your own law, see to it yourselves. I do not wish to be a judge of such matters." ¹⁶And he drove them away from the tribunal. ¹⁷They all seized Sosthenes, the synagogue official, and beat him in full view of the tribunal. But none of this was of concern to Gallio.

Return to Syrian Antioch

¹⁸Paul remained for quite some time, and after saying farewell to the brothers he sailed for Syria, together with Priscilla and Aquila. At Cenchreae he had his hair cut because he had taken a vow.

continue

18:1-17 Paul in Corinth

Because the New Testament contains two of the letters that Paul later wrote to the Christian community in Corinth, we know more about this community than any of the other churches that Paul founded. The correspondence that we call 1 and 2 Corinthians gives us a privileged window on the texture and tensions of this vibrant community in the middle fifties of the first century. In the first half of Acts 18, Luke, apparently working from sources other than Paul's letters, sketches the beginnings of that fascinating church. Some of the strokes of that sketch provide precious contact with historical data; other strokes limn Luke's inspired interpretation of those events, showing what God is doing through human failures and successes in that busy crossroads of the ancient world.

Acts 18 offers two important links with secular history. The Roman historian Suetonius tells us that the emperor Claudius expelled members of the Jewish community of Rome because of an "uproar" caused by one "Chrestus" in A.D. 49. Scholars have taken that to be a garbled reference to *Christos*. It would seem to refer to a stir caused by Jewish Christians from Jerusalem preaching Jesus as the Messiah. Priscilla and Aquila, then, seem to be part of that group expelled from Rome. They are "Jews for Jesus" who host Christian meetings at their house (1 Cor 16:19), as they will later do in Rome, when Nero allows Jews to return five years later (see Rom 16:5). This enterprising couple takes in as houseguest Paul, their fellow tentmaker and messianic missioner. An inscription found at Delphi dates the proconsul of Achaia, Gallio, to A.D. 51–52, thus providing another link to secular history.

But it is sacred history that most interests Luke. He shows that the whim of an emperor and the adjudication of a proconsul can play into the divine project. Aquila and Prisca (Priscilla) become two of Paul's principal co-workers, and their hospitality enables the Apostle to settle into what was (next to his twenty-seven-month stay in Ephesus; see 19:10) his second most extended sojourn in a single town, lasting some eighteen months.

Paul's extended sessions at the local Jewish house of study, with Gentile God-fearers as well as Jews in attendance, issue in the usual mixed results. Most Jews reject the novelty of a crucified craftsman proclaimed as the Messiah and "the Lord." But there are notable exceptions: Crispus, the synagogue leader, and one Titus Justus, the God-fearer who owned the house next door to the synagogue. Paul's work is affirmed by a night vision of Jesus assuring him in language that recalls the divine promise of support to the prophets Isaiah and Jeremiah ("I am with you").

Tellingly, the mixed Christian community is called the Lord's "people" (*laos*, the biblical word for the people of the covenant; source of our word "laity"). When Paul's Jewish adversaries bring him before the bench of the proconsul Gallio, he unwittingly affirms that "covenantal peoplehood" of the Christians by dismissing their charges against Paul as a matter of Jewish doctrine, titles, and law (v. 15).

[19]When they reached Ephesus, he left them there, while he entered the synagogue and held discussions with the Jews. [20]Although they asked him to stay for a longer time, he did not consent, [21]but as he said farewell he promised, "I shall come back to you again, God willing." Then he set sail from Ephesus. [22]Upon landing at Caesarea, he went up and greeted the church and then went down to Antioch. [23]After staying there some time, he left and traveled in orderly sequence through the Galatian country and Phrygia, bringing strength to all the disciples.

Apollos

[24]A Jew named Apollos, a native of Alexandria, an eloquent speaker, arrived in Ephesus. He was an authority on the scriptures. [25]He had been instructed in the Way of the Lord and, with ardent

continue

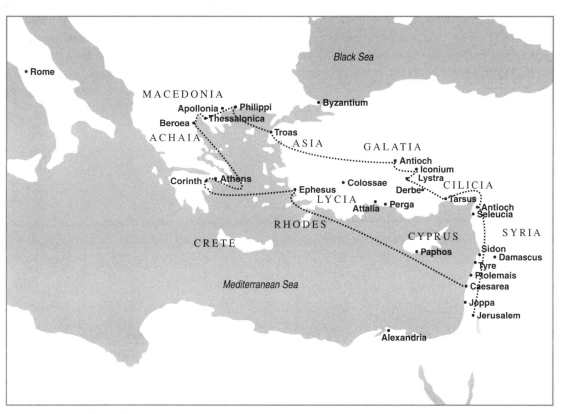

Second Journey of Paul (Acts 15:36–18:22)

spirit, spoke and taught accurately about Jesus, although he knew only the baptism of John. ²⁶He began to speak boldly in the synagogue; but when Priscilla and Aquila heard him, they took him aside and explained to him the Way [of God] more accurately. ²⁷And when he wanted to cross to Achaia, the brothers encouraged him and wrote to the disciples there to welcome him. After his arrival he gave great assistance to those who had come to believe through grace. ²⁸He vigorously refuted the Jews in public, establishing from the scriptures that the Messiah is Jesus.

18:18-28 Further mission notes and the integration of Apollos

Luke's intent in the remainder of chapter 18 seems mainly to give a summary of activity occurring between Paul's work in Corinth and his work in another major urban center, Ephesus (to be treated in Acts 19). The résumé highlights features that are key to Luke's interpretation. (1) Paul continues to operate as a Jew (see the reference to the Nazirite haircut, v. 18; for background, see Num 6:1-21). (2) He continues his mission to fellow Jews (he dialogues with the Ephesian synagogue congregation).

(3) He stays in touch with church officials at the Jerusalem headquarters (v. 22). (4) The Christian mission continues in an orderly way. For example, Paul revisits and affirms communities established in Phrygia and Galatia. And when Apollos, a skilled rhetorician from the Hellenistic Christian/Jewish community of Alexandria, arrives in Ephesus and begins to preach the "Way of the Lord" with enthusiasm, but incompletely, Paul's co-workers, Priscilla and Aquila, explain the Way to him more fully. Apollos's move from Ephesus to Achaia is done with the recommendation of the Ephesian Christians.

 Apollos was a co-worker of Paul and was highly esteemed by the Corinthian community (1 Cor 1:12; 3:4). Only Acts records any biographical information about him (18:24-28).

(The power of Apollos's ministry was such that some of those he trains will form a kind of "I had the great Apollos as my personal trainer" faction, and Paul will have to address this issue in 1 Corinthians 1–3. See especially 1 Corinthians 3:6: "I planted, Apollos watered, but *God* caused the growth," emphasis added).

EXPLORING LESSON ONE

1. Although Paul and Barnabas part ways before embarking on a second missionary journey, both men continue to be committed to the work of evangelization (15:36-41). How do you overcome personality differences or practical obstacles in carrying out your role as a disciple?

_____

_____

_____

_____

_____

2. The decision of the early church leaders at the Council of Jerusalem is to forego the requirement of circumcision for Gentile believers (15:28-29). What is Paul's purpose, then, in having Timothy circumcised (16:3)?

_____

_____

_____

_____

_____

3. What is the significance of the use of "we" in several parts of Acts (16:10-17; 20:5-15; 21:1-18; 27:1–28:16)?

_____

_____

_____

_____

_____

4. The story of Paul's encounter with Lydia (16:11-15, 40) is an example of how Paul forged relationships with people who were open to God's work in their lives. What relationships in your life are rooted in a particular way in your shared love for Jesus?

_____

_____

_____

_____

_____

5. a) What is the charge against Paul and Silas when they are arrested in Philippi (16:20-23)?

_____

_____

_____

_____

_____

b) In spite of their suffering, what good results come from their arrest (16:25-39)?

_____

_____

_____

_____

6. Paul and Silas reportedly spend three weeks among the Jewish community in Thessalonica, preaching, teaching, and getting to know people (17:1-4). In a world that favors instant gratification and quick results, what lessons might we learn? (See Gal 6:9; Rom 12:12.)

_____

_____

_____

_____

_____

7. a) In what ways does Paul adapt his preaching to the Athenians (17:22-31)? Why does he make these adaptations?

_____

_____

_____

_____

_____

b) Why do some of the philosophers sneer at Paul after they listen attentively (17:32)? (See 1 Cor 15:12-19.)

_____

_____

_____

_____

8. What teaching of Jesus comes to mind when reading about Paul's reaction to the Jews in 18:5-6? (See Matt 10:11-14.)

_____

_____

_____

_____

_____

_____

9. Why does Gallio refuse to hear the case against Paul (18:12-16)?

_____

_____

_____

_____

_____

10. Review the ways that Priscilla and Aquila help the cause of the gospel (18:1-3, 18, 26; see also Rom 16:3; 1 Cor 16:19; 2 Tim 4:19). What avenues are open to those in your community to promote the work of the gospel?

_____

_____

_____

_____

_____

_____

CLOSING PRAYER

Prayer

"He made from one the whole human race to dwell on the entire surface of the earth, and he fixed the ordered seasons and the boundaries of their regions, so that people might seek God, even perhaps grope for him and find him, though indeed he is not far from any one of us." (Acts 17:26-27)

Creator of all that is and will be, we turn to you, humbled by your desire that all people come to know you. Allow each person to encounter you in our world: through nature, acts of generosity, intellectual searching, and our witness to your love. We pray this day that we will become creative in our words and deeds so that people will discover that you are near indeed. Today we pray for the courage to reach out to those who do not seem to know you yet, especially . . .

LESSON TWO

Acts 19–21

Begin your personal study and group discussion with a simple and sincere prayer such as:

Prayer

   God of the Universe, we marvel at those who first carried the good news to the far reaches of the earth. Allow these sacred readings to encourage us to carry the gospel into the world where we live.

Read the Bible text of Acts 19–21 found in the outside columns of pages 28–38, highlighting what stands out to you.

Read the accompanying commentary to add to your understanding.

Respond to the questions on pages 39–41, Exploring Lesson Two.

The Closing Prayer on page 42 is for your personal use and may be used at the end of group discussion.

CHAPTER 19

Paul in Ephesus

¹While Apollos was in Corinth, Paul traveled through the interior of the country and came [down] to Ephesus where he found some disciples. ²He said to them, "Did you receive the holy Spirit when you became believers?" They answered him, "We have never even heard that there is a holy Spirit." ³He said, "How were you baptized?" They replied, "With the baptism of John." ⁴Paul then said, "John baptized with a baptism of repentance, telling the people to believe in the one who was to come after him, that is, in Jesus." ⁵When they heard this, they were baptized in the name of the Lord Jesus. ⁶And when Paul laid [his] hands on them, the holy Spirit came upon them, and they spoke in tongues and prophesied. ⁷Altogether there were about twelve men.

⁸He entered the synagogue, and for three months debated boldly with persuasive arguments about the kingdom of God. ⁹But when some in their obstinacy and disbelief disparaged the Way

continue

19:1-40 Paul in Ephesus: the Way of the Lord Jesus versus magic and idolatry; evangelizing from the Asian capital (19:1-12)

Paul's encounter with twelve Ephesian "disciples" who had not received the holy Spirit provides an instructive parallel with the previous episode—Priscilla and Aquila's instruction of Apollos. Both involve the instruction of disciples who are somehow incomplete. Apollos's incompleteness was subtle: although he had been instructed in the Way of the Lord (vv. 25-26; see 9:2; 14:16; 16:17) and taught accurately about Jesus and was ardent in spirit, he knew only the baptism of John, was not described as filled with the Spirit, and needed to be taught *more* accurately about the Way. Similarly, these twelve Ephesians, who seem to have missed the training of Aquila, Priscilla, and the reformed

Apollos, also knew only John's baptism and had not even heard that there was a holy Spirit.

As in the case of the conversion of Cornelius's household (10:44-46), a "mini-Pentecost" follows. These two descriptions of "regularizing" disciples tell us two interesting things about the emergent church: (a) that the influence of John the Baptist was more powerful than we usually give him credit for, and (b) unity of belief and practice within the church had been a struggle from the beginning.

The summary description in verses 8-12 portrays the shape of the next twenty-seven months of Paul's evangelization. Despite past rejections, his serious effort to bring the good news to his fellow Jews first continues with a three-month colloquium in the Ephesian synagogue. That this effort was not entirely without success is hinted at in the reference to the *disciples* whom Paul took with him after a nasty confrontation compelled him to change his venue to the hall of Tyrannus.

During the next two years Ephesus becomes a mission center from which the whole province of Asia is evangelized, "Jews and Greeks alike." The description of healings occasioned even by cloth or aprons touched to Paul's skin demonstrates that the healing ministry begun in Jesus (Luke 8:44-47, the woman with the flow of blood) and continued through Peter (Acts

5:15-16) persists in the Apostle to the Gentiles. See Paul's own reference to his work as "what Christ has accomplished through me to lead the Gentiles to obedience by word and deed, by the power of signs and wonders . . ." (Rom 15:18-19; see also 2 Cor 12:12).

19:13-20 The power of Jesus' name versus demons and magic

The power of the risen Lord Jesus over the competing powers of this world is now illustrated by two vivid and entertaining anecdotes regarding demons, magic, and idolatry.

When the seven sons of the high priest Sceva attempt to deliver a man from demonic oppression by using Jesus' name in a magical way, they themselves are rebuked, overpowered, and sent packing, naked and wounded. The spiritual power of the name of the Lord Jesus, properly used, is dramatized by the immense commercial value of books burned by those converted from their magical practices (v. 19).

before the assembly, he withdrew and took his disciples with him and began to hold daily discussions in the lecture hall of Tyrannus. [10]This continued for two years with the result that all the inhabitants of the province of Asia heard the word of the Lord, Jews and Greeks alike. [11]So extraordinary were the mighty deeds God accomplished at the hands of Paul [12]that when face cloths or aprons that touched his skin were applied to the sick, their diseases left them and the evil spirits came out of them.

The Jewish Exorcists

[13]Then some itinerant Jewish exorcists tried to invoke the name of the Lord Jesus over those with evil spirits, saying, "I adjure you by the Jesus whom Paul preaches." [14]When the seven sons of Sceva, a Jewish high priest, tried to do this, [15]the

continue

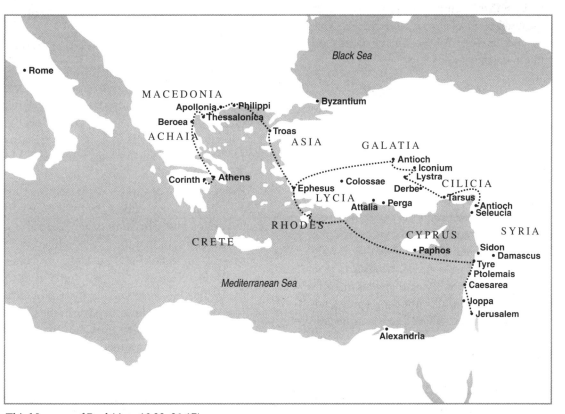

Third Journey of Paul (Acts 18:23–21:17)

evil spirit said to them in reply, "Jesus I recognize, Paul I know, but who are you?" [16]The person with the evil spirit then sprang at them and subdued them all. He so overpowered them that they fled naked and wounded from that house. [17]When this became known to all the Jews and Greeks who lived in Ephesus, fear fell upon them all, and the name of the Lord Jesus was held in great esteem. [18]Many of those who had become believers came forward and openly acknowledged their former practices. [19]Moreover, a large number of those who had practiced magic collected their books and burned them in public. They calculated their value and found it to be fifty thousand silver pieces. [20]Thus did the word of the Lord continue to spread with influence and power.

Paul's Plans

[21]When this was concluded, Paul made up his mind to travel through Macedonia and Achaia, and then to go on to Jerusalem, saying, "After I have been there, I must visit Rome also." [22]Then he sent to Macedonia two of his assistants, Timothy and Erastus, while he himself stayed for a while in the province of Asia.

The Riot of the Silversmiths

[23]About that time a serious disturbance broke out concerning the Way. [24]There was a silversmith named Demetrius who made miniature silver shrines of Artemis and provided no little work for the craftsmen. [25]He called a meeting of these and other workers in related crafts and said, "Men, you know well that our prosperity derives from this work. [26]As you can now see and hear, not only in Ephesus but throughout most of the province of Asia this Paul has persuaded and misled a great number of people by saying that gods made by hands are not gods at all. [27]The danger grows, not only that our business will be discredited, but also that the temple of the great goddess Artemis will be of no account, and that she whom the whole province of Asia and all the world worship will be stripped of her magnificence."

continue

19:21-40 A confused assembly confronted

The Way of the Lord Jesus continues to have practical consequences. The silversmiths of Ephesus riot when their livelihood (selling silver models of the world-famous temple of the goddess Artemis) appears to be threatened by the Christian preaching against idolatry. (Archaeology helps us to picture the structures involved here. One of the "seven wonders of the ancient world," the temple of Artemis, the Artemision, was four times the size of the Parthenon, with 127 sixty-foot pillars. The dimensions alone help us understand why silver models of the place were such hot items in the religious tourism trade. And the "theater" was not like your local movie house but a magnificent amphitheater carved into a mountainside, 495

Statue of Artemis

feet in diameter.) Two important points emerge from Luke's account of this disruption. First, the intervention of the town clerk models the way for Roman officials to work out tensions with Christians: ("let the matter be settled in the lawful assembly," v. 39).

Second, some of Luke's word choices hint that he is making a subtle contrast between pagan chaos and Christian order. Describing the riot, Luke says that the city was filled with *synchysis* ("confusion"—v. 29). Used only once in the New Testament, this is a deftly chosen word, for it is the word used in the Septuagint at Genesis 11:9 (the sole occurrence in the Greek version of the Torah) to translate the name "Babel." And Luke has already used the verbal form of the word to describe the Pentecost experience as a reversal of Babel's confusion (Acts 2:6), Pentecost being the occasion when people are confused by their ability to understand!

The contrast is further enhanced by Luke's using *ekklēsia* to describe the confused assembly in verses 32, 39, and 41. Apart from Acts 7:38, where the word refers to the assembly of the Hebrews at Sinai, *ekklēsia* elsewhere in Acts always means the community of the church. Only in this passage is the word used for a non-ecclesial assembly. For the original readers of Acts, this word choice could only have pointed up the contrast between the two kinds of "assembly"—the confused riot of the silversmiths versus the orderly growth of the church (vv. 10-17, 20). The final two occurrences of *ekklēsia* in Acts turn up in the very next chapter, in verses 17 and 28, where they describe the Ephesian church as an assembly driven by motives quite other than idolatry, greed, and anxiety.

Paul spent more than two years ministering in the cosmopolitan seaport **city of Ephesus**. Located near modern Kushadasi in Turkey, it is one of the most important archaeological sites of the New Testament world. Archaeological finds there have helped to fill in many details of urban life in the first century including artifacts used in everyday life, the structures of sumptuous houses of the rich, foundations of shops and apartments in the market area, and excellently preserved theaters and remnants of pagan temples.

The main street in Ephesus at one time led directly to the port.

[28]When they heard this, they were filled with fury and began to shout, "Great is Artemis of the Ephesians!" [29]The city was filled with confusion, and the people rushed with one accord into the theater, seizing Gaius and Aristarchus, the Macedonians, Paul's traveling companions. [30]Paul wanted to go before the crowd, but the disciples would not let him, [31]and even some of the Asiarchs who were friends of his sent word to him advising him not to venture into the theater. [32]Meanwhile, some were shouting one thing, others something else; the assembly was in chaos, and most of the people had no idea why they had come together. [33]Some of the crowd prompted Alexander, as the Jews pushed him forward, and Alexander signaled with his hand that he wished to explain something to the gathering. [34]But when they recognized that he was a Jew, they all shouted in unison, for about two hours, "Great is Artemis of the Ephesians!" [35]Finally the town clerk restrained the crowd and said, "You Ephesians, what person is there who does not know that the city of the Ephesians is the guardian of the temple of the great Artemis and of her image that fell from the sky? [36]Since these things are undeniable, you must calm yourselves and not do anything rash. [37]The men you brought here are not temple robbers, nor have they insulted our goddess. [38]If Demetrius and his fellow craftsmen have a complaint against anyone, courts are in session, and there are proconsuls. Let them bring charges against one another. [39]If you have anything further to investigate, let the matter be settled in the lawful assembly, [40]for, as it is, we are in danger of being charged with rioting because of today's conduct. There is no cause for it. We shall [not] be able to give a reason for this demonstration." With these words he dismissed the assembly.

CHAPTER 20

Journey to Macedonia and Greece

[1]When the disturbance was over, Paul had the disciples summoned and, after encouraging them,

continue

he bade them farewell and set out on his journey to Macedonia. ²As he traveled throughout those regions, he provided many words of encouragement for them. Then he arrived in Greece, ³where he stayed for three months. But when a plot was made against him by the Jews as he was about to set sail for Syria, he decided to return by way of Macedonia.

Return to Troas

⁴Sopater, the son of Pyrrhus, from Beroea, accompanied him, as did Aristarchus and Secundus from Thessalonica, Gaius from Derbe, Timothy, and Tychicus and Trophimus from Asia ⁵who went on ahead and waited for us at Troas. ⁶We sailed from Philippi after the feast of Unleavened Bread, and rejoined them five days later in Troas, where we spent a week.

Eutychus Restored to Life

⁷On the first day of the week when we gathered to break bread, Paul spoke to them because he was going to leave on the next day, and he kept on speaking until midnight. ⁸There were many lamps in the upstairs room where we were gathered, ⁹and a young man named Eutychus who was sitting on the window sill was sinking into a deep sleep as Paul talked on and on. Once overcome by sleep, he fell down from the third story and when he was picked up, he was dead. ¹⁰Paul went down, threw himself upon him, and said as he embraced him, "Don't be alarmed; there is life in him." ¹¹Then he returned upstairs, broke the bread, and ate; after a long conversation that lasted until daybreak, he departed. ¹²And they took the boy away alive and were immeasurably comforted.

Journey to Miletus

¹³We went ahead to the ship and set sail for Assos where we were to take Paul on board, as he had arranged, since he was going overland. ¹⁴When he met us in Assos, we took him aboard and went on to Mitylene. ¹⁵We sailed away from there on the next day and reached a point off Chios, and a day later we reached Samos, and on the following

continue

20:1-16 Journeying toward Jerusalem (and the resuscitation of "Lucky")

In a note between the episodes of the triumph over the exorcists and the riot of the silversmiths (19:21), Luke had already referred to Paul's decision to travel to Jerusalem (and then move on to Rome). Although Paul later (24:17) refers to the purpose of this journey as the bringing of alms to Jerusalem (the collection referred to in his letters to Corinth and Rome—for instance, Romans 15:25-28), there is no mention of the collection here in chapter 20. Perhaps the delivery of the Jerusalem relief fund was not the public-relations success Paul had hoped for.

After a farewell tour of churches in Macedonia and three months in "Greece" (Achaia, centering, no doubt, around unnamed Corinth), Paul, intending to join what was apparently a pilgrim group of Jews sailing for Syria, learns of a plot against him and decides to take a more indirect route, looping back around the Aegean basin. The seven names listed (plus the author or his source, since the second "we" section begins in verse 5) comprise a delegation representing most of the sectors of Paul's mission. This delegation fits the notion that this is indeed the "Jerusalem relief fund" trip (see Rom 15:25-27).

The colorful anecdote about the resuscitation of Eutychus (aptly named "Lucky," the meaning of his name in Greek) may well be included here simply for its entertainment value and its parallel with the account of Peter's raising of Tabitha (9:36-43). But given Luke's careful choice of words and phrases— "on the first day of the week" (v. 7; see Luke 24:1); "upstairs room" (v. 8; see 1:13; 9:37, 39); "break[ing] bread" (vv. 7, 11; see Luke 22:19; 24:30; Acts 2:46); a fallen youth taken up "dead" (v. 9) and revived by Paul imitating the gestures of Elijah and Elisha and taken away as a *pais zōnta* ("living lad"), it is hard to dismiss the possibility that the author intends the reader to reflect on the story's symbolic resonances, especially when one notices that the event sits between references to Passover ("the feast of Unleavened Bread," v. 6) and Pentecost

(v. 16). For the Christian practice of the breaking of the bread on the first day of the week (Sunday) is always a celebration of death and restoration to new life, precisely as these things are interpreted in the light of the Jewish feasts of Passover and Pentecost.

As for the detailed itinerary surrounding this anecdote, the listing of places could simply be explained as evidence of an eyewitness's passion for detail. It could also reflect Luke's intention to show how Jesus' heroic follower Paul imitates his master even in his making an extended final journey to Jerusalem, where he too will be interrogated by Jewish and Gentile officials.

Eutychus himself is not the focus of the story in Acts 20:7-12. However, his situation provides the framework for considering the value of shared faith, the power of the spoken word, the potential of the gathered community, and the significance of breaking bread together. "There is life in him" is the message of Christianity. Physical life, emotional life, spiritual life, mental life—in all these ways we can bear witness to the effects of the gospel message in our midst.

20:17-38 Paul's testament to the Ephesian elders

Paul makes a point of bypassing Ephesus (to avoid those plotting against him?), but he is eager to summon the elders of that community to Miletus, some forty miles to the south, so that he can bid them farewell. What follows is the only speech in Acts that Paul addresses to a Christian audience.

The speech follows the conventions of other biblical testaments, touching on the topics of a review of the speaker's life, commissioning of successors, encouragement and warnings regarding the future, farewell and blessing. Like other classic farewell addresses, it serves both to present the speaker as a model for the readers/auditors and also to address the historical

day we arrived at Miletus. ¹⁶Paul had decided to sail past Ephesus in order not to lose time in the province of Asia, for he was hurrying to be in Jerusalem, if at all possible, for the day of Pentecost.

Paul's Farewell Speech at Miletus

¹⁷From Miletus he had the presbyters of the church at Ephesus summoned. ¹⁸When they came to him, he addressed them, "You know how I lived among you the whole time from the day I first came to the province of Asia. ¹⁹I served the Lord with all humility and with the tears and trials that came to me because of the plots of the Jews, ²⁰and I did not at all shrink from telling you what was for your benefit, or from teaching you in public or in your homes. ²¹I earnestly bore witness for both Jews and Greeks to repentance before God and to faith in our Lord Jesus. ²²But now, compelled by the Spirit, I am going to Jerusalem. What will happen to me there I do not know, ²³except that in one city after another the holy Spirit has been warning me that imprisonment and hardships await me. ²⁴Yet I consider life of no importance to me, if only I may finish my course and the ministry that I received from the Lord Jesus, to bear witness to the gospel of God's grace.

²⁵"But now I know that none of you to whom I preached the kingdom during my travels will ever see my face again. ²⁶And so I solemnly declare to you this day that I am not responsible for the blood of any of you, ²⁷for I did not shrink from proclaiming to you the entire plan of God. ²⁸Keep watch over yourselves and over the whole flock of which the holy Spirit has appointed you overseers, in which you tend the church of God that he acquired with his own blood. ²⁹I know that after my departure savage wolves will come among you, and they will not spare the flock. ³⁰And from your own group, men will come forward perverting the truth to draw the disciples away after them. ³¹So be vigilant and remember that for three years, night and day, I unceasingly admonished each of you with tears. ³²And now I commend you to God and to that gracious word of his that can build you up and

continue

aftermath of the speaker and interpret what is going forward historically.

In the context of Luke-Acts, the speech is a privileged moment in Paul's own imitation of Christ. Like Jesus, he makes his own "passion prediction" on the way to Jerusalem. And his farewell address to the Ephesian elders has much in common with Jesus' own farewell address to the apostles at the Last Supper (Luke 22:25-38). Like Jesus at the supper, Paul characterizes authority in the messianic community as one of humble service, focuses on the kingdom, encourages his listeners to care for those left in their charge (Jesus: "Strengthen your brothers"; Paul: "Help the weak"), and warns of future challenges. That Paul can serve as model to the extent that he himself has imitated

Jesus is suggested by explicit reference to Jesus in the beatitude that climaxes the speech: "It is more blessed to give than to receive" (v. 35).

Several things about the language of this speech are worth noting. Along with Luke's calling the group "presbyters" (*presbyteroi*, or "elders," v. 17), the usual term in Acts for leaders other than the apostles in the churches, Paul calls them "overseers" (v. 28, translating *episkopoi*, the word rendered "bishops" in later Christian writings). This reflects the apparent equivalence of those terms as found, for example, in Titus 1:5-7. In the ordinary Greek of the day, *episkopos* meant "superintendent" or "guardian" in any of a variety of social settings. In first-century Christian writings it serves as a Hellenistic equivalent of the more Judean

Paul's farewell to the Ephesian elders

term "elder," which Luke uses for both Jewish and Christian leaders throughout Luke-Acts. In the second century these terms will be used to designate distinct roles in the evolving three-tier hierarchical structure of a single local bishop (*episkopos*), directing a number of elders (*presbyteroi*, from which the English words "priest" and "presbyterate" derive), supported by a further group of *diakonoi*, or deacons.

One remarkable verse (v. 28) deserves special attention: "Keep watch over yourselves and over the whole flock of which the holy Spirit has appointed you overseers, in which you tend the church of God that he acquired with his own blood." This translation, which renders straightforwardly what scholars generally agree is the best reading of the Greek text, raises the question of what it can mean to speak of God's blood. An early response to this problem was the introduction of the variant reading "church of the Lord" for "church of God," which was open to the understanding that "his blood" referred to the blood of the Lord Jesus. But the more difficult reading, "church of God," does appear to be the more authentic one. A possible solution of this crux is to translate the final phrase, "the blood of his Own" (referring to the Son, Jesus). In any case, with the references to "holy Spirit," "God," and "blood," we have in this verse a rare New Testament foreshadowing of the later, more developed doctrine of the Trinity. Using phrases that catch important aspects of Paul's theology as it is expressed in the Pauline letters (conversion to God, faith in the Lord Jesus, the power of the Spirit to form community, the gospel of God's grace, the plan of God, the importance of perseverance), this speech is a fitting conclusion to Luke's narrative of Paul's intra-Christian ministry.

21:1-14 Paul and the delegation continue the journey to Jerusalem

After departing from Ephesus, Paul and companions continue the journey to Jerusalem. This stage of the journey comprises the third "we" section in Acts (vv. 1-18), implying the author's presence during this part of the journey. The summary gives us a glimpse of how

give you the inheritance among all who are consecrated. [33]I have never wanted anyone's silver or gold or clothing. [34]You know well that these very hands have served my needs and my companions. [35]In every way I have shown you that by hard work of that sort we must help the weak, and keep in mind the words of the Lord Jesus who himself said, 'It is more blessed to give than to receive.'"

[36]When he had finished speaking he knelt down and prayed with them all. [37]They were all weeping loudly as they threw their arms around Paul and kissed him, [38]for they were deeply distressed that he had said that they would never see his face again. Then they escorted him to the ship.

CHAPTER 21

Arrival at Tyre

[1]When we had taken leave of them we set sail, made a straight run for Cos, and on the next day for Rhodes, and from there to Patara. [2]Finding a ship crossing to Phoenicia, we went on board and put out to sea. [3]We caught sight of Cyprus but passed by it on our left and sailed on toward Syria and put in at Tyre where the ship was to unload cargo. [4]There we sought out the disciples and stayed for a week. They kept telling Paul through the Spirit not to embark for Jerusalem. [5]At the end of our stay we left and resumed our journey. All of them, women and children included, escorted us out of the city, and after kneeling on the beach to pray, [6]we bade farewell to one another. Then we boarded the ship, and they returned home.

continue

people got about the Mediterranean in those days: they hung around a port until they found a cargo ship going in the general direction of their intended destination.

The fact that Paul and his entourage find communities of Christians in Tyre and Ptolemais indicates that the evangelization of Phoenicia, to which Luke referred in 11:19, took root and flourished. Indeed, the intensity of communion

Arrival at Ptolemais and Caesarea

[7]We continued the voyage and came from Tyre to Ptolemais, where we greeted the brothers and stayed a day with them. [8]On the next day we resumed the trip and came to Caesarea, where we went to the house of Philip the evangelist, who was one of the Seven, and stayed with him. [9]He had four virgin daughters gifted with prophecy. [10]We had been there several days when a prophet named Agabus came down from Judea. [11]He came up to us, took Paul's belt, bound his own feet and hands with it, and said, "Thus says the holy Spirit: This is the way the Jews will bind the owner of this belt in Jerusalem, and they will hand him over to the Gentiles." [12]When we heard this, we and the local residents begged him not to go up to Jerusalem. [13]Then Paul replied, "What are you doing, weeping and breaking my heart? I am prepared not only to be bound but even to die in Jerusalem for the name of the Lord Jesus." [14]Since he would not be dissuaded we let the matter rest, saying, "The Lord's will be done."

Paul and James in Jerusalem

[15]After these days we made preparations for our journey, then went up to Jerusalem. [16]Some of the disciples from Caesarea came along to lead us to the house of Mnason, a Cypriot, a disciple of long standing, with whom we were to stay. [17]When we reached Jerusalem the brothers welcomed us warmly. [18]The next day, Paul accompanied us on a visit to James, and all the presbyters were present. [19]He greeted them, then proceeded

continue

when Agabus, who prophesied accurately the famine during the reign of Claudius (Acts 11:28), acts out symbolically what he perceives to be the Spirit's message regarding Paul's fate in Jerusalem, he gets it only partly right: Paul will indeed be bound in Jerusalem, but by Romans, not by Jews. Faced with Paul's determination to go to Jerusalem even if it means death, it is the companions, not Paul, who imitate Jesus' struggle in facing the prospect of death (Luke 22:39-42), first with resistance, then acceptance.

21:15-26 Paul has his Jewish fidelity challenged

When Paul and company arrive in Jerusalem, James and a plenary session of the Jerusalem elders hear Paul's report about what God has been doing through his ministry among the Gentiles. The Jerusalem Christian authorities are happy enough with that good news, but they inform Paul that the success among the Gentiles has raised concerns among the "many thousands" (v. 20) of Jewish Christians in the area who have gotten the idea that he is urging all the Jews in the Diaspora to abandon the Mosaic practices. Although nothing we have read in Acts supports this charge, Paul's own letter to the Romans shows that the notion that he was denigrating the Mosaic law was prevalent enough to warrant the full-scale defense that he makes in that major letter.

James's strategy for damage control in this regard—having Paul accompany four men to the temple and sponsor the ceremonies fulfilling their nazirite vows (see Num 6:3-20 for the nazirite ritual)—seems promising. Twentieth-century digs to the south of the Temple Mount have revealed the *mikvaot* (immersion baths), where pilgrims ritually purified themselves before climbing the stairs leading up into the temple precincts. The public nature of this purification, along with Paul's sponsoring of the sacrifices (twelve animals, three apiece for four men) would offer a clear rebuttal to the accusations that Paul was discouraging observance of the Torah.

The reference in verse 25 to the policy regarding Gentile converts expressed in the ap-

with the disciples at Ptolemais is enough to warrant the same kind of prayerful seaside send-off they received at Ephesus (20:36-38).

These episodes illustrate that hearing and following the Spirit are not a simple matter. Although the Tyrian Christians keep telling Paul "through the Spirit" not to embark for Jerusalem, he continues. Obviously, he feels they have misinterpreted the Spirit in this case. And

ostolic decree of the Jerusalem Council (Acts 15:23-29) strikes an odd note here. Paul, after all, played a major part in that meeting and, indeed, helped promulgate its policy regarding Gentile converts (16:4). But the notice serves to remind the reader that the present issue, Paul's attitude toward Jewish observance of the Torah, is something other than what is expected of Gentile Christians.

Given Paul's own language about "[dying] to the law" (Gal 2:19), some commentators find Luke's portrayal here of Paul's "compromise" implausible. Yet it can be argued that Paul is acting in a way wholly consistent with the policy he articulates in 1 Corinthians 9:19-21: "Although I am free in regard to all, I have made myself a slave to all so as to win over as many as possible. To the Jews I became like a Jew to win over Jews; to those under the law I became like one under the law—though I myself am not under the law—to win over those under the law. To those outside the law I became like one outside the law—though I am not outside God's law but within the law of Christ—to win over those outside the law."

Sadly, in the end the strategy fails, for in the events that follow, nothing indicates that Paul's Jerusalem relief fund was accepted, and no one in the Jerusalem Christian community comes to his rescue in the confrontation that continues to unfold. The Jerusalem church, so robustly present in the early chapters of Acts and now grown to "many thousands," disappears from view during the final seven chapters.

21:27-36 Romans rescue Paul from an attempted lynching

In addition to the local members of the sect of the Nazarene, other Jews, pilgrims from the province of Asia, mount an attack against Paul. Having recognized their fellow provincial, the Gentile Trophimus, some had jumped to the conclusion that Paul had taken this man into the court of Israel on the Temple Mount, thereby breaching the barrier separating Gentiles from the space reserved for Israelites. Signs posted on the balustrade forbade Gentiles to pass this point on pain of death. The

to tell them in detail what God had accomplished among the Gentiles through his ministry. [20]They praised God when they heard it but said to him, "Brother, you see how many thousands of believers there are from among the Jews, and they are all zealous observers of the law. [21]They have been informed that you are teaching all the Jews who live among the Gentiles to abandon Moses and that you are telling them not to circumcise their children or to observe their customary practices. [22]What is to be done? They will surely hear that you have arrived. [23]So do what we tell you. We have four men who have taken a vow. [24]Take these men and purify yourself with them, and pay their expenses that they may have their heads shaved. In this way everyone will know that there is nothing to the reports they have been given about you but that you yourself live in observance of the law. [25]As for the Gentiles who have come to believe, we sent them our decision that they abstain from meat sacrificed to idols, from blood, from the meat of strangled animals, and from unlawful marriage." [26]So Paul took the men, and on the next day after purifying himself together with them entered the temple to give notice of the day when the purification would be completed and the offering made for each of them.

Paul's Arrest

[27]When the seven days were nearly completed, the Jews from the province of Asia noticed him in the temple, stirred up the whole crowd, and laid hands on him, [28]shouting, "Fellow Israelites, help us. This is the man who is teaching everyone everywhere against the people and the law and this place, and what is more, he has even brought Greeks into the temple and defiled this sacred place." [29]For they had previously seen Trophimus the Ephesian in the city with him and supposed that Paul had brought him into the temple. [30]The whole city was in turmoil with people rushing together. They seized Paul and dragged him out of the temple, and immediately the gates were closed. [31]While they were trying to kill him, a

continue

report reached the cohort commander that all Jerusalem was rioting. ³²He immediately took soldiers and centurions and charged down on them. When they saw the commander and the soldiers they stopped beating Paul. ³³The cohort commander came forward, arrested him, and ordered him to be secured with two chains; he tried to find out who he might be and what he had done. ³⁴Some in the mob shouted one thing, others something else; so, since he was unable to ascertain the truth because of the uproar, he ordered Paul to be brought into the compound. ³⁵When he reached the steps, he was carried by the soldiers because of the violence of the mob, ³⁶for a crowd of people followed and shouted, "Away with him!"

³⁷Just as Paul was about to be taken into the compound, he said to the cohort commander, "May I say something to you?" He replied, "Do you speak Greek? ³⁸So then you are not the Egyptian who started a revolt some time ago and led the four thousand assassins into the desert?" ³⁹Paul answered, "I am a Jew, of Tarsus in Cilicia, a citizen of no mean city; I request you to permit me to speak to the people." ⁴⁰When he had given his permission, Paul stood on the steps and motioned with his hand to the people; and when all was quiet he addressed them in Hebrew.

rioting crowd falls upon Paul, haul him out of the sacred space, and try to kill him on the spot.

At this point the cohort commander intervenes with centurions and soldiers, who bring him to "the compound," a reference to the Antonia fortress, the military headquarters and barracks contiguous with the northwest corner of the temple platform. The shout of the crowd—"Away with him!"—echoes the cry at the trial of Jesus before Pilate (Luke 23:18).

21:37-40 Paul identifies himself

When Paul identifies himself as a Jew and a Roman citizen to the cohort commander, the latter is relieved that he is not "the Egyptian"— the last rabble-rouser the Romans had to deal with. The reference fits Josephus's account of an "Egyptian false prophet" who, a few years earlier, had led thirty thousand (Josephus's number) to the Mount of Olives to wait for Jerusalem to fall like Jericho in the days of Joshua. Paul and his purpose are something else entirely, as his ensuing speech will reveal. Having spoken to the commander in Greek, the *lingua franca* of that part of the empire, he now proceeds to address the crowd in what Luke calls "Hebrew"—almost certainly a reference to Aramaic, the mother tongue of Jesus and the common language of Judea.

EXPLORING LESSON TWO

1. What can we learn about the way the early church evangelized and then catechized (instructed in the faith) from the stories of Apollos and the disciples Paul found in Ephesus (18:24-28; 19:1-7)?

_____

_____

_____

_____

_____

2. Acts includes a number of references to "the Way" (9:2; 18:25-26; 19:9, 23; 22:4; 24:22). What might be the basis for referring to the followers of Jesus with this title? (See Matt 22:16; Mark 1:2-3; John 14:1-6.)

_____

_____

_____

_____

_____

3. Paul says that he desires to visit Rome, the capital of the empire (19:21). What can we learn about his reasons from reading Romans 1:8-15 and 15:22-32?

_____

_____

_____

_____

_____

4. The silversmiths in Ephesus perceive the preaching of Paul and his companions as a threat to their livelihood of supplying statues of the shrine of Artemis to citizens and tourists (19:23-40), reminding us that sometimes Christian values are at odds with local economies. Can you think of any examples of this? How do these conflicts raise important questions for people of faith?

_____

_____

_____

_____

5. a) What is the feast of Unleavened Bread (20:6)? (See Exod 12:1-17.)

_____

_____

_____

_____

_____

   b) What significance might there be to the mention of this feast before Eutychus is restored to life, and to the mention of Pentecost after he is restored (20:16)?

_____

_____

_____

_____

_____

6. How does the content of Paul's speech to the Christian elders from Ephesus (20:17-35) compare with some of the content of letters associated with Paul? (See 1 Cor 9:24; Phil 1:20-21; 2 Tim 4:7.)

_____

_____

_____

_____

_____

_____

7. Here in Acts as well as in his letters, Paul is clear that he works for his wages (Acts 20:33-55; 1 Cor 4:11-12; 9:6-12; 1 Thess 2:9; 2 Thess 3:8). What does Paul's attitude toward work say about the value of human labor? (See also 2 Thess 3:7-10.)

_____

_____

_____

_____

_____

_____

8. Apparently, Paul's work among the Gentiles made him the subject of rumors and even opened him to false accusations that he taught Jewish believers to no longer adhere to Jewish law (21:15-21). How do the Christian leaders in Jerusalem help Paul try to quash any ill will or false rumors (21:22-32)? Are they successful?

_____

_____

_____

_____

_____

_____

9. Paul's work outside of Jewish territory was misunderstood and misinterpreted. In what ways do you believe our faith may be misunderstood today? What factors contribute to this?

_____

_____

_____

_____

_____

_____

10. What is the reason for Paul's arrest by the cohort commander in Jerusalem (21:33)?

_____

_____

_____

_____

_____

_____

CLOSING PRAYER

Prayer
"The Lord's will be done." (Acts 21:14)

We pray this day, O Lord, that we will embrace your will in our lives, not as a burden to be carried or a resolve to be shouldered, but in the sure knowledge that your way leads to glory. Give us both courage and joy as we seek your will in our lives. Today, we pray especially for insights about your will for us . . .

LESSON THREE

Acts 22–24

Begin your personal study and group discussion with a simple and sincere prayer such as:

Prayer

God of the Universe, we marvel at those who first carried the good news to the far reaches of the earth. Allow these sacred readings to encourage us to carry the gospel into the world where we live.

Read the Bible text of Acts 22–24 found in the outside columns of pages 44–50, highlighting what stands out to you.

Read the accompanying commentary to add to your understanding.

Respond to the questions on pages 51–53, Exploring Lesson Three.

The Closing Prayer on page 54 is for your personal use and may be used at the end of group discussion.

CHAPTER 22

Paul's Defense before the Jerusalem Jews

[1]"My brothers and fathers, listen to what I am about to say to you in my defense." [2]When they heard him addressing them in Hebrew they became all the more quiet. And he continued, [3]"I am a Jew, born in Tarsus in Cilicia, but brought up in this city. At the feet of Gamaliel I was educated strictly in our ancestral law and was zealous for God, just as all of you are today. [4]I persecuted this Way to death, binding both men and women and delivering them to prison. [5]Even the high priest and the whole council of elders can testify on my behalf. For from them I even received letters to the brothers and set out for Damascus to bring back to Jerusalem in chains for punishment those there as well.

[6]"On that journey as I drew near to Damascus, about noon a great light from the sky suddenly shone around me. [7]I fell to the ground and heard a voice saying to me, 'Saul, Saul, why are you persecuting me?' [8]I replied, 'Who are you, sir?' And he said to me, 'I am Jesus the Nazorean whom you are persecuting.' [9]My companions saw the light but did not hear the voice of the one who spoke to me. [10]I asked, 'What shall I do, sir?' The Lord answered me, 'Get up and go into Damascus, and there you will be told about everything appointed for you to do.' [11]Since I could see nothing because of the brightness of that light, I was led by hand by my companions and entered Damascus.

[12]"A certain Ananias, a devout observer of the law, and highly spoken of by all the Jews who lived there, [13]came to me and stood there and said, 'Saul, my brother, regain your sight.' And at that very moment I regained my sight and saw him. [14]Then he said, 'The God of our ancestors designated you to know his will, to see the Righteous One, and to hear the sound of his voice; [15]for you will be his witness before all to what you have seen and heard. [16]Now, why delay? Get up and have yourself baptized and your sins washed away, calling upon his name.'

[17]"After I had returned to Jerusalem and while I was praying in the temple, I fell into a trance

continue

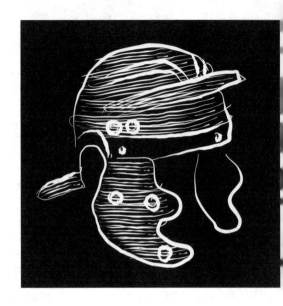

22:1-21 Paul's first defense speech

Paul's exchange with the cohort commander had raised questions of ethnicity and status. Paul is a Jew, not "the Egyptian." He speaks Greek as well as Aramaic. And he is a Roman citizen. Now as he begins his speech, he makes it clear that he speaks as a Jew to Jews ("My brothers and fathers"). The clause "what I am about to say . . . in my defense" renders the word *apologia*, the classical term for a legal defense, thereby setting the agenda for the final seven chapters of Acts. Facing a crowd driven by zeal for the Mosaic law—who are attacking Paul because they think he has violated that law—he makes the perfect move to win their good will. He displays his Jewish pedigree, citing his Jewish upbringing, his training in the law, even describing his own past persecution of "this Way" as stemming from precisely the "zeal . . . for God" that they are presently demonstrating in their persecution of him.

Just as Luke repeated twice the story of Peter's first mission to Gentiles in his encounter with Cornelius's household (in Acts 10, 11, and 15), so he retells the story of Paul's conversion/commission here, for the second in what will be another series of three accounts. No clumsy redundancy, these repetitions are the author's way of underscoring the importance of these pivotal events. As in the case of Peter's encounter with Cornelius, each retelling comes with variations and developments that fit the immediate context and help the reader fathom the significance more deeply.

In this version of Paul's encounter with the risen Jesus, the brightness is enhanced: at the most brilliant time of day, *noon*, Paul experiences a brightness that outshines the noontime sunlight! His visual impairment is not called blindness here but is simply ascribed to the brightness of the light. Whereas in the account of Acts 9 the companions hear the voice but see no one, here they see the light but hear no voice.

These are not the discrepancies of a negligent author but variations of an artist in full control of his material. Saying that "the Lord" answered Paul enhances the nature of the vision as a theophany, that is, a manifestation of God. (It is not impossible that Luke's emphasis on blindness in the midst of brightness is prompted by his perception that Paul here experiences the noontime blindness that Deuteronomy 28:28 promises Israel if it does not hearken to the voice of the Lord.)

The Jewishness of Ananias is enhanced. He is a "devout observer of the law" (v. 12). And he announces that their ancestral God has designated Paul to witness (what he had seen and heard) "before *all*" (emphasis added) about "the Righteous One," an eminently Jewish title for Jesus, denoting fidelity to the covenant and echoing Luke's unique version of the confession of the centurion under the cross (Luke 23:47: "This man was *dikaios*" ["innocent," "righteous"]). Here there is less emphasis on the physical cure from blindness; restored vision simply follows upon Ananias's word.

If Paul's adversaries are challenging his mission to Gentiles, the final part of the speech claims that the outreach to the nations was far from the action of an apostate. Like the great prophet Isaiah, Paul "saw the Lord" in the temple, protested his unworthiness, and received his mandate there, at the liturgical heart of Israel (v. 18; see Isa 6:1). In response, the crowd repeats the rejection of 21:36.

---

[18] and saw the Lord saying to me, 'Hurry, leave Jerusalem at once, because they will not accept your testimony about me.' [19] But I replied, 'Lord, they themselves know that from synagogue to synagogue I used to imprison and beat those who believed in you. [20] And when the blood of your witness Stephen was being shed, I myself stood by giving my approval and keeping guard over the cloaks of his murderers.' [21] Then he said to me, 'Go, I shall send you far away to the Gentiles.'"

Paul Imprisoned

[22] They listened to him until he said this, but then they raised their voices and shouted, "Take such a one as this away from the earth. It is not right that he should live." [23] And as they were yelling and throwing off their cloaks and flinging dust into the air, [24] the cohort commander ordered him to be brought into the compound and gave instruction that he be interrogated under the lash to determine the reason why they were making such an outcry against him. [25] But when they had stretched him out for the whips, Paul said to the centurion on duty, "Is it lawful for you to scourge a man who is a Roman citizen and has not been tried?" [26] When the centurion heard this, he went to the cohort commander and reported it, saying, "What are you going to do? This man is a Roman citizen." [27] Then the commander came and said to

continue

22:22-29 Paul imprisoned

Just as the tribune was caught in a false assumption about Paul earlier (that he was "the Egyptian," 21:38), now he is caught in another mistake about the Apostle's identity—assuming that this Jew is not a Roman citizen. Wrong again. This vivid drama, with Paul stretched out for interrogation under the lash and then rescued at the last minute, is more than good storytelling. It also demonstrates for Luke's readership that Paul, as a Roman citizen, is eminently qualified to mediate the gospel to the Roman world as well as to the Diaspora.

him, "Tell me, are you a Roman citizen?" "Yes," he answered. ²⁸The commander replied, "I acquired this citizenship for a large sum of money." Paul said, "But I was born one." ²⁹At once those who were going to interrogate him backed away from him, and the commander became alarmed when he realized that he was a Roman citizen and that he had had him bound.

Paul before the Sanhedrin

³⁰The next day, wishing to determine the truth about why he was being accused by the Jews, he freed him and ordered the chief priests and the whole Sanhedrin to convene. Then he brought Paul down and made him stand before them.

CHAPTER 23

¹Paul looked intently at the Sanhedrin and said, "My brothers, I have conducted myself with a perfectly clear conscience before God to this day." ²The high priest Ananias ordered his attendants to strike his mouth. ³Then Paul said to him, "God will strike you, you whitewashed wall. Do you indeed sit in judgment upon me according to the law and yet in violation of the law order me to be struck?" ⁴The attendants said, "Would you revile God's high priest?" ⁵Paul answered, "Brothers, I did not realize he was the high priest. For it is written, 'You shall not curse a ruler of your people.'"

⁶Paul was aware that some were Sadducees and some Pharisees, so he called out before the Sanhedrin, "My brothers, I am a Pharisee, the son of Pharisees; [I] am on trial for hope in the resurrection of the dead." ⁷When he said this, a dispute broke out between the Pharisees and Sadducees, and the group became divided. ⁸For the Sadducees say that there is no resurrection or angels or spirits, while the Pharisees acknowledge all three. ⁹A great uproar occurred, and some scribes belonging to the Pharisee party stood up and sharply argued, "We find nothing wrong with this man. Suppose a spirit or an angel has spoken to him?" ¹⁰The dispute was so serious that the commander, afraid that Paul

continue

Citizenship in the ancient Mediterranean world was originally a simple description of one's place of birth or residence. By the time of the Roman Empire, citizenship came to be associated with male privilege in the city of Rome, and eventually throughout the empire. Citizenship was usually acquired by birth or by service to the empire, though sometimes as a result of adoption or freedom from slavery. Once acquired, citizenship was passed through one's family. During the time of the first-century church, Roman citizens enjoyed, among other rights, the right to a fair trial (Acts 16:37), exemption from torture (22:25), and appeal to the emperor (25:11). Such rights gradually eroded as the Roman Empire decayed.

22:30–23:11 The investigation continues: Paul before the Sanhedrin

Having learned of Paul's Roman citizenship, the commander (Claudius Lysias, we learn in verse 26) tries a gentler mode of getting to the facts of the charges against Paul. He orders the chief priests and the full Sanhedrin to convene for a hearing. Notice that these people are not necessarily gathered as adversaries of Paul; they comprise the official Jewish body that the commander now looks to in order to discover whether Paul is a danger to Roman law and order. Thus we are not yet dealing with a trial; Lysias is still conducting a Roman investigation to see if Paul has done something that warrants a Roman trial.

Paul's declaration that he has always conducted himself with a clear conscience before God surely applies to his whole life and supports the notion that his experience on the road to Damascus is better understood as a prophetic call rather than a conversion, at least in the moral or religious sense.

The exchange between Paul and the high priest Ananias is loaded with irony. Paul comes across as a better exponent of the law than does its official guardian. His assertion that he did not realize Ananias was the high priest implies that the latter's behavior, punishing an unconvicted person, was hardly the deportment expected of a person in that office.

Before any formal inquest begins, Paul asserts that he is a Pharisee (v. 6) and makes a simple proclamation of the gospel: "[I] am on trial for the hope in the resurrection of the dead." Commentators note Paul's shrewdness in playing the afterlife card, a key point of division between the two parties. As Jesus' controversy with the Sadducees in Luke 20:27-40 demonstrated, Sadducees denied the resurrection. And as Luke notes here in a rare aside, neither did they believe in postmortem survival as "angel" or "spirit." For the Sadducees, if you could not find it in the Torah, it didn't count. This, of course, splits the Sanhedrin, with the Pharisees refusing to condemn Brother Paul.

 Flavius **Josephus** (ca. A.D. 37–100) was a Jewish scholar and historian whose written works serve as credible sources of information about many events in Jewish history. By extension, from his writings we learn much about the political and social realities of the New Testament era. Josephus's tome, *The Antiquities of the Jews*, includes one of the earliest references to Jesus outside of the New Testament.

would be torn to pieces by them, ordered his troops to go down and rescue him from their midst and take him into the compound. [11]The following night the Lord stood by him and said, "Take courage. For just as you have borne witness to my cause in Jerusalem, so you must also bear witness in Rome."

Transfer to Caesarea

[12]When day came, the Jews made a plot and bound themselves by oath not to eat or drink until they had killed Paul. [13]There were more than forty who formed this conspiracy. [14]They went to the chief priests and elders and said, "We have bound ourselves by a solemn oath to taste nothing until we have killed Paul. [15]You, together with the Sanhedrin, must now make an official request to the commander to have him bring him down to you, as though you meant to investigate his case more thoroughly. We on our part are prepared to kill him before he arrives." [16]The son of Paul's sister, however, heard about the ambush; so he went and entered the compound and reported it to Paul. [17]Paul then called one of the centurions and requested, "Take this young man to the commander; he has something to report to him." [18]So he took him and brought him to the commander and explained, "The prisoner Paul called me and asked that I bring this young man to you; he has

continue

But more is going on here than clever forensic strategy. By the time of Luke's writing of Acts, the high priest Ananias has indeed been "struck," assassinated in A.D. 66, according to Josephus. The Sadducees have ceased to exist as authorities, having lost their power base with the destruction of the temple by the Romans in A.D. 70. This leaves the Pharisees, the current leaders of formative Judaism, as the most important figures for Luke's readers. They emerge in this episode not so much as defenders of Paul but rather as men acting in

bad will. Though they accept "the resurrection of the dead" as a hope, they resist Paul's testimony that the hoped-for resurrection has already begun concretely in Jesus of Nazareth.

It is this, rather than Paul's legal guilt or innocence, that will remain the issue for the remainder of the book. It is really the gospel that is on trial. In the context of the narrative, Paul's focus on the resurrection makes it clear to the Roman tribune (the most important auditor of this hearing) that the charges against Paul are Jewish matters, nothing of concern to imperial governance.

something to say to you." ¹⁹The commander took him by the hand, drew him aside, and asked him privately, "What is it you have to report to me?" ²⁰He replied, "The Jews have conspired to ask you to bring Paul down to the Sanhedrin tomorrow, as though they meant to inquire about him more thoroughly, ²¹but do not believe them. More than forty of them are lying in wait for him; they have bound themselves by oath not to eat or drink until they have killed him. They are now ready and only wait for your consent." ²²As the commander dismissed the young man he directed him, "Tell no one that you gave me this information."

²³Then he summoned two of the centurions and said, "Get two hundred soldiers ready to go to Caesarea by nine o'clock tonight, along with seventy horsemen and two hundred auxiliaries. ²⁴Provide mounts for Paul to ride and give him safe conduct to Felix the governor." ²⁵Then he wrote a letter with this content: ²⁶"Claudius Lysias to his excellency the governor Felix, greetings. ²⁷This man, seized by the Jews and about to be murdered by them, I rescued after intervening with my troops when I learned that he was a Roman citizen. ²⁸I wanted to learn the reason for their accusations against him so I brought him down to their Sanhedrin. ²⁹I discovered that he was accused in matters of controversial questions of their law and not of any charge deserving death or imprisonment. ³⁰Since it was brought to my attention that there will be a plot against the man, I am sending him to you at once, and have also notified his accusers to state [their case] against him before you."

³¹So the soldiers, according to their orders, took Paul and escorted him by night to Antipatris. ³²The next day they returned to the compound, leaving the horsemen to complete the journey with him. ³³When they arrived in Caesarea they delivered the letter to the governor and presented Paul to him. ³⁴When he had read it and asked to what province he belonged, and learned that he was from Cilicia, ³⁵he said, "I shall hear your case when your accusers arrive." Then he ordered that he be held in custody in Herod's praetorium.

continue

23:12-35 A plot to assassinate Paul and a Roman rescue

A group of more than forty of Paul's co-religionists make a pact not to eat or drink until they have killed him. Luke offers no motive for such fanaticism. One can only surmise that these men exhibit the kind of rebellious zealotry that will come to expression some ten years later in the Zealot revolt against Rome in A.D. 67–70. They may have perceived in Paul's messianic mission to the Gentiles (and his rumored "watering down" of Jewish practices) a vitiation, or undermining of Judean nationalism.

The **Zealots** were a Jewish sect characterized by opposition to Roman occupation of Judea and belief that a coming messiah would restore Jewish independence. They were known to employ violent tactics against their enemies and even against fellow Jews whom they believed were accommodating to Rome. The historian Josephus reports that the Zealots were the chief proponents of the Jewish rebellion against Rome that began in A.D. 66 and eventually led to the destruction of the Jerusalem temple in A.D. 70.

Tipped off by Paul's nephew regarding the plot to ambush his prisoner (v. 16), Lysias moves to place him in the protective custody of an armed cavalry, who are to escort him safely to the governor Felix (in office A.D. 52–59, the sixth prefect after Pontius Pilate).

Luke gives us the gist of the report Lysias sends to Felix. Given that our author has already provided his version of the events reported in the message, Luke no doubt expects the reader to smile at the way this Roman official tweaks the truth to put the best possible face on his conduct. We know from 21:27-40 that Lysias first quelled the riot, arrested Paul, and eventually ordered him interrogated under the lash. Only *then*, when Paul announced his citizenship, did the tribune first learn of it. As Lysias tells it in his report, his action with Paul was from the beginning a bold rescue of a known Roman citizen. In his favor, his present "protective custody" action has in fact become such a rescue.

We may wonder why Felix, when he learns that Paul is from Cilicia, does not send him there for trial. In fact, Syria-Cilicia is a double province at this time (Vespasian will split it later), and Felix governs the area in which the charges have been brought against the accused. So he is responsible for the trial.

24:1-27 Paul is heard before Felix, in public and privately

Finally, with the arrival from Jerusalem of Ananias and some elders with their attorney, Paul faces a formal trial before the procurator Felix. After paying unctuous compliments to the governor, Tertullus, the prosecuting attorney, levels a set of broad and, as we readers know, unfounded charges against Paul: (a) he sows dissension among Jews all over the world [empire] (*oikoumenē*) and (b) he tried to profane the temple. Tertullus even tries to dignify with the term "arrest" (v. 6) what we know to have been an attempt at mob lynching.

 Felix was a provincial procurator (or governor) of Judea from approximately A.D. 52–59. Procurators were appointed by the Roman emperor and were usually selected from among the senators or wealthy, aristocratic families with ties to the emperor. Their primary duties were keeping law and order, judging legal cases, and overseeing the collection of Roman taxes in their provinces.

As in his speech on the Antonia barracks steps to the crowd of would-be lynchers (Acts 22), Paul answers these false charges by rehearsing the facts that establish his exemplary and eminently traditional Jewish behavior. Far from desecrating the temple, he went there to worship their ancestral God. He is still a Torah-keeping Jew who worships the God he has always served

CHAPTER 24

Trial before Felix

[1]Five days later the high priest Ananias came down with some elders and an advocate, a certain Tertullus, and they presented formal charges against Paul to the governor. [2]When he was called, Tertullus began to accuse him, saying, "Since we have attained much peace through you, and reforms have been accomplished in this nation through your provident care, [3]we acknowledge this in every way and everywhere, most excellent Felix, with all gratitude. [4]But in order not to detain you further, I ask you to give us a brief hearing with your customary graciousness. [5]We found this man to be a pest; he creates dissension among Jews all over the world and is a ringleader of the sect of the Nazoreans. [6]He even tried to desecrate our temple, but we arrested him. [7] [8]If you examine him you will be able to learn from him for yourself about everything of which we are accusing him." [9]The Jews also joined in the attack and asserted that these things were so.

[10]Then the governor motioned to him to speak and Paul replied, "I know that you have been a judge over this nation for many years and so I am pleased to make my defense before you. [11]As you can verify, not more than twelve days have passed since I went up to Jerusalem to worship. [12]Neither in the temple, nor in the synagogues, nor anywhere in the city did they find me arguing with anyone or instigating a riot among the people. [13]Nor can they prove to you the accusations they are now making against me. [14]But this I do admit to you, that according to the Way, which they call a sect, I worship the God of our ancestors and I believe everything that is in accordance with the law and written in the prophets. [15]I have the same hope in God as they themselves have that there will be a resurrection of the righteous and the unrighteous. [16]Because of this, I always strive to keep my conscience clear before God and man. [17]After many years, I came to bring alms for my nation and offerings. [18]While I was so engaged, they found me,

continue

49

after my purification, in the temple without a crowd or disturbance. ¹⁹But some Jews from the province of Asia, who should be here before you to make whatever accusation they might have against me—²⁰or let these men themselves state what crime they discovered when I stood before the Sanhedrin, ²¹unless it was my one outcry as I stood among them, that 'I am on trial before you today for the resurrection of the dead.'"

²²Then Felix, who was accurately informed about the Way, postponed the trial, saying, "When Lysias the commander comes down, I shall decide your case." ²³He gave orders to the centurion that he should be kept in custody but have some liberty, and that he should not prevent any of his friends from caring for his needs.

Captivity in Caesarea

²⁴Several days later Felix came with his wife Drusilla, who was Jewish. He had Paul summoned and listened to him speak about faith in Christ Jesus. ²⁵But as he spoke about righteousness and self-restraint and the coming judgment, Felix became frightened and said, "You may go for now; when I find an opportunity I shall summon you again." ²⁶At the same time he hoped that a bribe would be offered him by Paul, and so he sent for him very often and conversed with him.

²⁷Two years passed and Felix was succeeded by Porcius Festus. Wishing to ingratiate himself with the Jews, Felix left Paul in prison.

in good conscience, except that now it is according to "the Way" that his adversaries dismiss as a "sect." Their charges are hearsay and therefore without merit. The original plaintiffs were the "Jews from . . . Asia" (21:27), but they are not present to testify. And the only thing that the present plaintiffs have witnessed was his proclamation that he is on trial "for the resurrection of the dead" (v. 21; see 23:6).

Paul's claim to have come "to bring alms for my nation and offerings" (v. 17) is the sole reference in Acts to his transmission of the Jerusalem relief fund (see Rom 15:25-26) as the main motive for his presence in Jerusalem. By calling the collection "alms for my nation" and linking it with his sponsoring of sacrifices for the nazirites fulfilling their vows, he casts those actions in language that associates them with the essence of Jewish piety. Felix's knowledge that Paul, as bearer of these funds, controls a substantial amount of money may well be what generated the governor's hope for a bribe (v. 26).

Since Felix is informed about "the Way" (through his Jewish wife Drusilla?), and since he has perhaps decided that the Way is no threat to Roman social order, he postpones judgment, pending further (unnecessary) consultation with Lysias. Felix allows two years to elapse without coming to judgment. Like most of the leaders in Luke-Acts, Jewish or Roman, Felix wants chiefly to look after his own interests. (Regarding Felix's administration, the Roman historian Tacitus observes, "He exercised the power of a king with the spirit of the slave.")

St. Paul in Prison, Rembrandt (1627)

EXPLORING LESSON THREE

1. What most Bibles refer to as Paul's "speech" or "discourse" to his fellow Jews in Jerusalem is more of a personal testimony about God in his life (22:1-21). What events would you include if you were called to give witness to how God has acted in your life?

_____

_____

_____

_____

_____

2. How does Paul use both his Jewish heritage and his Roman citizenship to his advantage in the events described in Acts 22?

_____

_____

_____

_____

_____

_____

3. Paul's questioning by the Sanhedrin opens with an exchange of insults. How does Paul then try to demonstrate that he is a good Jew and obedient to the law (23:1-5)? (See Exod 22:27.)

_____

_____

_____

_____

4. Paul is both honest and clever. How does he split the Sanhedrin and manage to escape punishment (23:6-11)? (See 4:1-2.)

_____

_____

_____

_____

_____

5. Because of the controversy surrounding Paul and the danger to his life, the cohort commander in Jerusalem intervenes and keeps him safe in the compound overnight. There Paul receives encouragement in the words of the Lord (23:10-11). What words of the Lord (perhaps favorite Bible stories or verses) have encouraged you in times of distress?

_____

_____

_____

_____

_____

_____

6. The crowd that is tempted to take justice into its own hands is certainly not the first to believe justice is better served by violence upon violence (23:12-15). How does your faith inform your views about punishment and violence? (See Prov 3:31; 16:29; Matt 5:38-39; 26:51-52; Luke 22:33-34; Rom 12:17-18; 1 Pet 3:9.)

_____

_____

_____

_____

_____

7. Why is Paul transferred to Caesarea (23:20-30)?

_____

_____

_____

_____

8. Tertullus lays out the charges against Paul in the hearing before the Roman procurator, Felix: "We found this man to be a pest; he creates dissension among Jews all over the world and is a ringleader of the sect of the Nazoreans. He even tried to desecrate our temple" (24:5-6). How do these charges sound to your ears?

_____

_____

_____

_____

9. In the two years Paul is imprisoned in Caesarea awaiting trial or some resolution to the charges against him, he speaks with Felix, the Roman procurator of the region, on several occasions. What could Paul have done to shorten his detention (24:24-27)?

_____

_____

_____

_____

_____

10. We know from other New Testament writings that Paul used his time in prison to write letters to communities he had established or visited. Which letters may have come from this time in Caesarea, or later imprisonments, is not certain. What is clear is that Paul does not cease to be an evangelist even when his typical ways of doing so are cut off. When have unforeseen circumstances given you an opportunity to exercise your faith in new ways?

_____

_____

_____

_____

_____

CLOSING PRAYER

Prayer

"I am on trial before you today for the resurrection of the dead." (Acts 24:21)

To life! This is the gospel message. You, Lord, make all things new. From seedlings that split open and die in order to sprout and then bear fruit, to your very body stretched on a cross, hidden in a tomb, only to rise again, you are about life! Should our lives be examined for evidence of faith, may we bear witness to life as the final word in all things. Take whatever is complacent in us, whatever is lazy or tired, and breathe life there so that your good news comes alive in our midst. This day we pray to be life-givers to those in our parish or families who are sad, lonely, or ill, and for all those in need of our care, especially . . .

LESSON FOUR

Acts 25–28

Begin your personal study and group discussion with a simple and sincere prayer such as:

Prayer

God of the Universe, we marvel at those who first carried the good news to the far reaches of the earth. Allow these sacred readings to encourage us to carry the gospel into the world where we live.

Read the Bible text of Acts 25–28 found in the outside columns of pages 56–67, highlighting what stands out to you.

Read the accompanying commentary to add to your understanding.

Respond to the questions on pages 68–70, Exploring Lesson Four.

The Closing Prayer on page 71 is for your personal use and may be used at the end of group discussion.

CHAPTER 25

Appeal to Caesar

[1]Three days after his arrival in the province, Festus went up from Caesarea to Jerusalem [2]where the chief priests and Jewish leaders presented him their formal charges against Paul. They asked him [3]as a favor to have him sent to Jerusalem, for they were plotting to kill him along the way. [4]Festus replied that Paul was being held in custody in Caesarea and that he himself would be returning there shortly. [5]He said, "Let your authorities come down with me, and if this man has done something improper, let them accuse him."

[6]After spending no more than eight or ten days with them, he went down to Caesarea, and on the following day took his seat on the tribunal and ordered that Paul be brought in. [7]When he appeared, the Jews who had come down from Jerusalem surrounded him and brought many serious charges against him, which they were unable to prove. [8]In defending himself Paul said, "I have committed no crime either against the Jewish law or against the temple or against Caesar." [9]Then Festus, wishing to ingratiate himself with the Jews, said to Paul in reply, "Are you willing to go up to Jerusalem and there stand trial before me on these charges?" [10]Paul answered, "I am standing before the tribunal of Caesar; this is where I should be tried. I have committed no crime against the Jews, as you very well know. [11]If I have committed a crime or done anything deserving death, I do not seek to escape the death penalty; but if there is no substance to the charges they are bringing against me, then no one has the right to hand me over to them. I appeal to Caesar." [12]Then Festus, after conferring with his council, replied, "You have appealed to Caesar. To Caesar you will go."

Paul before King Agrippa

[13]When a few days had passed, King Agrippa and Bernice arrived in Caesarea on a visit to Festus. [14]Since they spent several days there, Festus referred Paul's case to the king, saying, "There is

continue

25:1-12 Paul appeals to Caesar and comes before Agrippa

This chapter of Acts functions mainly as a transition. Luke is setting the scene for Paul's climactic speech before Agrippa in chapter 26. As he does so, he strengthens two themes important to his history: (a) the controversy regarding Paul and the Christian Way is a thoroughly Jewish matter, and (b) the legal structure and personnel of the Roman Empire are functioning at this time as instruments of Divine Providence.

When Jewish leaders present their (now two-year-old) case against Paul and request that he be sent to them in Jerusalem (to be ambushed and killed along the way), Festus asserts his imperial authority. If they have charges to bring against a man in Roman custody, let them do it on the procurator's turf, before his tribunal in Caesarea (v. 5). Luke reflects Paul's adversaries' charges in Paul's response: he has done nothing against the Torah or against the temple *or against Caesar*. "Against Caesar" is a new note, paralleling the charges of the Sanhedrin against Jesus before Pilate (Luke 23:2). When Festus offers Paul the option of facing a formal trial before the Sanhedrin in Jerusalem, he appeals to Caesar. This allows Festus to unburden himself of this case, and he decides to send Paul to Rome.

25:13-27 Paul before Agrippa

Enter King Agrippa and his twice-widowed sister Bernice. Agrippa—Herod Agrippa II—is the fourth Herod to appear in Luke's work. Herod the Great, the famous builder of Caesarea and Masada and spectacular renovator of the Second Temple, reigned at the time of the infancies of John the Baptist and Jesus (Luke 1:5). Herod the Tetrarch (Antipas), son of Herod the Great, ruled Galilee and Perea during the rest of Jesus' life. Herod Agrippa I (ruled A.D. 41–44), grandson of Herod the Great, appeared (and died) in Acts 12. Now we meet the great-grandson, Herod Agrippa II (who ruled after A.D. 50). We learn nothing new in Festus's report to Agrippa, but the way the report is expressed is telling. Festus characterizes the elders' charges as entirely a Jewish affair—"some issues . . . about their own religion"—much as Gallio spoke when he dismissed the Corinthian Jews' quarrel with Paul in Acts 18:15 and as Lysias wrote in his report to Felix (23:29). There is a nice irony in the title used for the emperor in v. 26. The Greek word that our NABRE translates (accurately, in this context) as "our sovereign" is *ho kyrios* (literally, "the lord"). Given that the last instance of that word was a title for the risen Jesus (23:11) and the next instance, a few verses later, again refers to Jesus (26:15), the use of the title here

a man here left in custody by Felix. [15]When I was in Jerusalem the chief priests and the elders of the Jews brought charges against him and demanded his condemnation. [16]I answered them that it was not Roman practice to hand over an accused person before he has faced his accusers and had the opportunity to defend himself against their charge. [17]So when [they] came together here, I made no delay; the next day I took my seat on the tribunal and ordered the man to be brought in. [18]His accusers stood around him, but did not charge him with any of the crimes I suspected. [19]Instead they had some issues with him about their own religion and about a certain Jesus who had died but who Paul claimed was alive. [20]Since I was at a loss how to investigate this controversy, I asked if he were willing to go to Jerusalem and there stand trial on these charges. [21]And when Paul appealed that he be held in custody for the Emperor's decision, I ordered him held until I could send him to Caesar." [22]Agrippa said to Festus, "I too should like to hear this man." He replied, "Tomorrow you will hear him."

[23]The next day Agrippa and Bernice came with great ceremony and entered the audience hall in the company of cohort commanders and the prominent men of the city and, by command of Festus, Paul was brought in. [24]And Festus said,

continue

(for Nero!) highlights the irony that the true lord of this history is not the emperor but Jesus—an irony that the book of Revelation will exploit richly.

When Festus invites Agrippa to interrogate Paul, it is not as a formal trial but rather as a hearing in the service of the Roman process; Festus hopes the Jewish king will come up with something substantive to report to Rome. This move also gives Luke the opportunity to underscore another parallel between the experience of the Apostle and his Master: as Procurator Pilate sent Jesus to the then current Jewish king (Herod Antipas) for a kind of

Caesar

"King Agrippa and all you here present with us, look at this man about whom the whole Jewish populace petitioned me here and in Jerusalem, clamoring that he should live no longer. ²⁵I found, however, that he had done nothing deserving death, and so when he appealed to the Emperor, I decided to send him. ²⁶But I have nothing definite to write about him to our sovereign; therefore I have brought him before all of you, and particularly before you, King Agrippa, so that I may have something to write as a result of this investigation. ²⁷For it seems senseless to me to send up a prisoner without indicating the charges against him."

CHAPTER 26

King Agrippa Hears Paul

¹Then Agrippa said to Paul, "You may now speak on your own behalf." So Paul stretched out his hand and began his defense. ²"I count myself fortunate, King Agrippa, that I am to defend myself before you today against all the charges made against me by the Jews, ³especially since you are an expert in all the Jewish customs and controversies. And therefore I beg you to listen patiently. ⁴My manner of living from my youth, a life spent from the beginning among my people and in Jerusalem, all [the] Jews know. ⁵They have known about me from the start, if they are willing to testify, that I have lived my life as a Pharisee, the strictest party of our religion. ⁶But now I am standing trial because of my hope in the promise made by God to our ancestors. ⁷Our twelve tribes hope to attain to that promise as they fervently worship God day and night; and on account of this hope I am accused by Jews, O king. ⁸Why is it thought unbelievable among you that God raises the dead? ⁹I myself once thought that I had to do many things against the name of Jesus the Nazorean, ¹⁰and I did so in Jerusalem. I imprisoned many of the holy ones with the authorization I received from the chief priests, and when they were to be put to death I cast my vote against

continue

hearing, so Procurator Festus presents Paul to another Jewish king. In Jesus' case, of course, Pilate was attempting to shunt the accused off to another jurisdiction. Festus, however, does not intend to let his charge slip out of Roman custody.

Verses 23-27 set the stage for Paul's final extended apologia in chapter 26. Luke packs the audience hall with an entourage that includes "cohort commanders and the prominent men of the city" (v. 23). Thus Paul will be addressing, along with Festus, Agrippa, and Bernice, powerful members of Caesarea's Gentile community.

26:1-23 The inquest before Governor Festus and King Agrippa

The speech that Paul gives to these powerful representatives of the Jewish and Gentile communities is, like the speeches in Acts 2, 3, 13, and 17, one of Luke's theological masterpieces. Much of what we denote by the post-biblical terms "ecclesiology" (theology of church), "Christology" (how Jesus is the Messiah), and "soteriology" (theory of salvation) Luke communicates through this speech.

First, Luke highlights Paul speaking as an expert Jew (a Pharisee, and therefore one highly trained in Israelite tradition) to a well-informed Jewish leader (Agrippa was completing the project of his great-grandfather, the renovation of the Second Temple). Moreover, Paul had demonstrated his zeal for his people's tradition in his efforts against what he had at first perceived as a threat to those traditions, the Way of the Jesus people. To top it off, the centerpiece of his teaching and preaching is the essence of Jewish hope—resurrection from the dead. The unmentioned novelty, of course, is that Paul and the rest of the people of the Way have been announcing that the expected end-time general resurrection has been stunningly anticipated by the resurrection of a single person, Jesus of Nazareth (see the reference to "the first to rise from the dead" at verse 23).

Paul then recounts for the second time the experience on the road to Damascus, making it the third time for us readers (who first heard of it in the original narrative of Acts 9 and then in the speech of Acts 22). The variations in the details and language in this third telling are far more than an effort at literary variety. The language about light, darkness, and seeing participates in a consistent symbolic theme carrying powerful implications.

 Acts recounts the **call or conversion of Paul** three times, highlighting its importance (9:1-19; 22:1-16; 26:12-18). The details in each account are not entirely consistent (e.g., the light, the voice, what the witnesses saw or heard), but all three accounts strongly affirm Paul's mission to the Gentiles.

This time the light from the sky *is brighter than the noonday sun*, flattening *everyone* to the ground. And the language about blindness—which was quite literally physical in the Acts 9 account, then muted in the Acts 22 version—is not even applied to Paul here. That imagery now describes the experience of Gentile converts. Here the emphasis is on the fact that Paul will witness to what he *has seen* and that he is being missioned to *open the eyes of the Gentiles* so that *they* may *turn from darkness to light*. Thus what Paul first experienced literally in his physical blindness in the first account becomes a metaphor for the Christian mission to the nations in this third account. This metaphor is developed further at the climax of the speech: Paul is saying "nothing different from what the prophets and Moses foretold, that the Messiah must suffer and that, as the first to rise from the dead, he would *proclaim light both to our people and to the Gentiles*" (vv. 22-23, emphasis added).

And how, precisely, does Luke understand that the risen Messiah "proclaims light" after the resurrection? The whole of Luke-Acts answers that question, especially in its use of quotations of Isaiah. At Luke 2:30-32, during the presentation in the temple, when Simeon takes the child Jesus into his arms and sings his famous *Nunc Dimittis,* he draws upon Isa-

them. ¹¹Many times, in synagogue after synagogue, I punished them in an attempt to force them to blaspheme; I was so enraged against them that I pursued them even to foreign cities.

¹²"On one such occasion I was traveling to Damascus with the authorization and commission of the chief priests. ¹³At midday, along the way, O king, I saw a light from the sky, brighter than the sun, shining around me and my traveling companions. ¹⁴We all fell to the ground and I heard a voice saying to me in Hebrew, 'Saul, Saul, why are you persecuting me? It is hard for you to kick against the goad.' ¹⁵And I said, 'Who are you, sir?' And the Lord replied, 'I am Jesus whom you are persecuting. ¹⁶Get up now, and stand on your feet. I have appeared to you for this purpose, to appoint you as a servant and witness of what you have seen [of me] and what you will be shown. ¹⁷I shall deliver you from this people and from the Gentiles to whom I send you, ¹⁸to open their eyes that they may turn from darkness to light and from the power of Satan to God, so that they may obtain forgiveness of sins and an inheritance among those who have been consecrated by faith in me.'

continue

iah's imagery of vision and light: "for my eyes have seen your salvation [LXX Isa 40:5] / which you prepared in sight of all the peoples, / a light for revelation to the Gentiles [Isa 42:6; 49:6], / and glory for your people Israel."

At his debut in Nazareth, Jesus employs LXX Isaiah 61:1-2 to characterize his mission, and the center of that quotation is "He has sent me to proclaim . . . recovery of sight to the blind" (Luke 4:18). Jesus does indeed give sight to the blind in the physical cure of the blind in his pre-Easter activity (Luke 7:21; 18:35-43), but it takes the post-Easter activity of the church in Acts to fulfill the promise of the Servant functioning as a light to the Gentiles. Luke makes that quite explicit when, at the synagogue in Pisidian Antioch, he has Paul and Barnabas (both!) say, "We now turn to the Gentiles. For

¹⁹"And so, King Agrippa, I was not disobedient to the heavenly vision. ²⁰On the contrary, first to those in Damascus and in Jerusalem and throughout the whole country of Judea, and then to the Gentiles, I preached the need to repent and turn to God, and to do works giving evidence of repentance. ²¹That is why the Jews seized me [when I was] in the temple and tried to kill me. ²²But I have enjoyed God's help to this very day, and so I stand here testifying to small and great alike, saying nothing different from what the prophets and Moses foretold, ²³that the Messiah must suffer and that, as the first to rise from the dead, he would proclaim light both to our people and to the Gentiles."

Reactions to Paul's Speech

²⁴While Paul was so speaking in his defense, Festus said in a loud voice, "You are mad, Paul; much learning is driving you mad." ²⁵But Paul replied, "I am not mad, most excellent Festus; I am speaking words of truth and reason. ²⁶The king knows about these matters and to him I speak boldly, for I cannot believe that [any] of this has escaped his notice; this was not done in a corner. ²⁷King Agrippa, do you believe the prophets? I know you believe." ²⁸Then Agrippa said to Paul, "You will soon persuade me to play the Christian." ²⁹Paul replied, "I would pray to God that sooner or later not only you but all who listen to me today might become as I am except for these chains."

³⁰Then the king rose, and with him the governor and Bernice and the others who sat with them. ³¹And after they had withdrawn they said to one another, "This man is doing nothing [at all] that deserves death or imprisonment." ³²And Agrippa said to Festus, "This man could have been set free if he had not appealed to Caesar."

CHAPTER 27

Departure for Rome

¹When it was decided that we should sail to Italy, they handed Paul and some other prisoners over to a centurion named Julius of the Cohort

continue

so the Lord has commanded us, 'I have made you a light to the Gentiles, that you may be an instrument of salvation to the ends of the earth'" (Acts 13:46-47; see Isa 49:6). Strikingly, language describing the Servant of Yahweh in Isaiah, earlier applied to Jesus by Simeon, is now applied to the post-Easter continuation of Jesus' mission by his followers. Thus when we hear the reference to the risen Christ proclaiming "light to the Gentiles" at the climax of Paul's speech in Acts 26, we know that what Paul and the rest of the church are doing is not only in continuity with Jesus' mission but their work is somehow the work of the risen Lord himself.

This was the import of Paul's vision on the road to Damascus ("Saul, Saul, why are you persecuting me?"—v. 14b). The risen Lord is identified with the believing community, and through them he opens the eyes of the nations and brings them from darkness to light. At the end of the book, Luke will have Paul use Isaiah 6:9-10 ("They have closed their eyes, / so that they may not see with their eyes") to characterize those of Israel who, like Saul before his conversion, fail to respond to the mission.

Whereas Festus responds to the defense simply with amazement ("You are mad, Paul") and Agrippa with cynicism, Festus, Bernice, and the rest comment that Paul is doing nothing that deserves death or imprisonment (v. 31). Thus, like Jesus (see Luke 23:4, 14, and 22), Paul is declared innocent three times by Roman officials and a Jewish king (Lysias, 23:29; Festus, 25:25; and Agrippa, 26:31-32). And also like (and with) Jesus, he is fulfilling Servant Israel's vocation to be a light to the nations.

27:1-44 To Rome: storm, shipwreck, and survival

As he nears the end of his history, Luke gives us a whopping good sea adventure. Some recent commentators have wondered why Luke, who can be so sparse in his treatment of such momentous events as, for example, the early spread of the Christian mission into the Hellenistic world (11:20-21), decides at this point to spend so much parchment on the details of Paul's voyage to Rome.

Some scholars, subscribing to the theory that the "we" sections are a literary convention and noting resonances with other ancient accounts of shipwreck, have suggested that Luke has imaginatively embellished some minimal facts available to him regarding Paul's voyage. Others, noting the abundance of nautical technical terms, posit that Luke took over an available voyage account and applied it to Paul.

It is, however, simpler and more reasonable to presume that Luke is sparse when his sources are sparse and that he willingly shares details when he has access to them, especially when he was an eyewitness to the events he describes. The first-person plural of this final "we" section (27:1–28:16) supports such an interpretation. Moreover, we have no evidence of the "we" form used as a literary convention in ancient history writing by authors who are not describing their own experience.

That Paul himself was richly experienced in sea travel and its dangers is clear from his

Augusta. [2]We went on board a ship from Adramyttium bound for ports in the province of Asia and set sail. Aristarchus, a Macedonian from Thessalonica, was with us. [3]On the following day we put in at Sidon where Julius was kind enough to allow Paul to visit his friends who took care of him. [4]From there we put out to sea and sailed around the sheltered side of Cyprus because of the headwinds, [5]and crossing the open sea off the coast of Cilicia and Pamphylia we came to Myra in Lycia.

Storm and Shipwreck

[6]There the centurion found an Alexandrian ship that was sailing to Italy and put us on board. [7]For many days we made little headway, arriving at Cnidus only with difficulty, and because the wind would not permit us to continue our course we sailed for the sheltered side of Crete off

continue

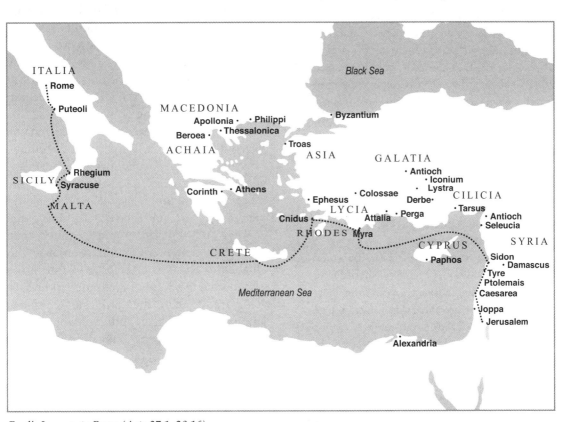

Paul's Journey to Rome (Acts 27:1–28:16)

Salmone. [8]We sailed past it with difficulty and reached a place called Fair Havens, near which was the city of Lasea.

[9]Much time had now passed and sailing had become hazardous because the time of the fast had already gone by, so Paul warned them, [10]"Men, I can see that this voyage will result in severe damage and heavy loss not only to the cargo and the ship, but also to our lives." [11]The centurion, however, paid more attention to the pilot and to the owner of the ship than to what Paul said. [12]Since the harbor was unfavorably situated for spending the winter, the majority planned to put out to sea from there in the hope of reaching Phoenix, a port in Crete facing west-northwest, there to spend the winter.

[13]A south wind blew gently, and thinking they had attained their objective, they weighed anchor and sailed along close to the coast of Crete. [14]Before long an offshore wind of hurricane force called a "Northeaster" struck. [15]Since the ship was caught up in it and could not head into the wind we gave way and let ourselves be driven. [16]We passed along the sheltered side of an island named Cauda and managed only with difficulty to get the dinghy under control. [17]They hoisted it aboard, then used cables to undergird the ship. Because of their fear that they would run aground on the shoal of Syrtis, they lowered the drift anchor and were carried along in this way. [18]We were being pounded by the storm so violently that the next day they jettisoned some cargo, [19]and on the third day with their own hands they threw even the ship's tackle overboard. [20]Neither the sun nor the stars were visible for many days, and no small storm raged. Finally, all hope of our surviving was taken away.

[21]When many would no longer eat, Paul stood among them and said, "Men, you should have taken my advice and not have set sail from Crete and you would have avoided this disastrous loss. [22]I urge you now to keep up your courage; not one of you will be lost, only the ship. [23]For last night an angel of the God to whom [I] belong and whom I serve stood by me [24]and said, 'Do not be afraid, Paul. You are destined to stand before Cae-

continue

remark in 2 Corinthians 11:25: "Three times I was shipwrecked, I passed a night and a day on the deep . . . ." And the tradition that Luke was a close companion of Paul is firm (Phlm 24; Col 4:14; and 2 Tim 4:11). There is no reason to presume that he was inexperienced in sea travel or lacked the vocabulary to describe it. Of course, master storyteller that he is, he knows he has a "good yarn" here. He tells it with relish and in a way that serves his history of what God has accomplished in and through these events, which could be called the passion and vindication of the Apostle Paul.

As a Roman citizen, Paul, accompanied by his faithful companion Aristarchus (see 19:29; 20:4; Col 4:10; and Phlm 24) and the narrator (presumably Luke), is placed under the protective custody of a centurion, one Julius. There being no commercial passenger ships in antiquity, Julius books passage on a ship returning to the Aegean area. The "philanthropic" (*philanthropos*) Julius allows Paul to visit friends, probably Christians, during a stop at Sidon. Because of the late fall weather, the ship hugs the coast, passing behind the shelter of Cyprus. At Myra they transfer to an Alexandrian grain ship headed for Italy. When they put in at Fair Havens, in the mid-south side of the island of Crete, Paul advises wintering there, since continuing now would entail loss of cargo and lives—reasonable advice that will turn out, in the end, to be only partly accurate.

When the voyage continues and a hurricane wind (a "northeaster") forces them dangerously off course, Paul provides quite a different sort of message. A dream vision enables him to urge courage and to predict (more accurately than his earlier commonsense prediction) safety to all aboard. The God he belongs to and serves would save them. It is significant that he says "God" rather than "the Lord Jesus" here; it is language that a pagan audience would more easily understand, and Luke is emphasizing that it is the maker of heaven and earth who is managing what is going forward in the midst of this chaos of nature.

Speaking of Luke's use of language, one cannot help noting that the description of Paul, acting in the manner of the host presiding at a Jewish meal (taking bread, thanking God, breaking the bread), evokes the language of the Last Supper and Christian Eucharist. Most commentators rightly insist that Luke surely does *not* mean to say that Paul, attended by his two Christian companions, is presiding at a Christian celebration of the Lord's Supper before a "congregation" of 273 pagans! At the same time, Luke the savvy wordsmith surely knows that his Christian readers (or hearers) would catch the resonance with the Christian liturgy (and with Luke 5:16 and 22:19).

Indeed, once that resonance is heard in verse 35, further resonances abound. For example:

1) Immediately before this mealtime blessing, Paul had said, "Not a hair of the head of anyone of you will be lost." This, of course, repeats what Jesus had said in his end-time discourse (Luke 21:18), which also speaks of "signs in the *sun, the moon, and the stars*," and asserts that "on earth nations will be in dismay, *perplexed by the roaring of the sea and the waves*" (Luke 21:25, emphasis added). In this literal experience of such a sea, Luke has made a point of noting that "neither the sun nor the stars were visible for many days" (Acts 27:20).

2) In a way that is more obvious in Greek than in English translation, Luke uses "salvation" language suggestively. The words used to describe physical survival of storm and shipwreck in this account (*sōzō* in vv. 20, 31; *sōtēria* in v. 34) are, to be sure, the usual words for describing rescue and survival; but in Luke's work, they are also used for salvation in the ultimate (eschatological) sense (e.g., *sōtēria*, "salvation," at Luke 1:77 [forgiveness of sins]; at 19:9 [Zacchaeus's conversion]; and at Acts 4:12; 13:26, 47; *sōtērion*, "salvation," at Luke 2:20 and 3:6 [Isa 40:5]; *sōzō*, the verbal form of "save," at Luke 7:50; 8:12; 13:23; 17:19; 18:26; 19:10; Acts 2:21 [Joel 3:5]; 2:47; 4:12; and 15:1, 11). That diction makes it easy, even inevitable, that readers will hear salvation overtones in the storm and shipwreck account of Acts 27.

3) Finally, in an extended work that has thematized the importance of detachment from

sar; and behold, for your sake, God has granted safety to all who are sailing with you.' ²⁵Therefore, keep up your courage, men; I trust in God that it will turn out as I have been told. ²⁶We are destined to run aground on some island."

²⁷On the fourteenth night, as we were still being driven about on the Adriatic Sea, toward midnight the sailors began to suspect that they were nearing land. ²⁸They took soundings and found twenty fathoms; a little farther on, they again took soundings and found fifteen fathoms. ²⁹Fearing that we would run aground on a rocky coast, they dropped four anchors from the stern and prayed for day to come. ³⁰The sailors then tried to abandon ship; they lowered the dinghy to the sea on the pretext of going to lay out anchors from the bow. ³¹But Paul said to the centurion and the soldiers, "Unless these men stay with the ship, you cannot be saved." ³²So the soldiers cut the ropes of the dinghy and set it adrift.

³³Until the day began to dawn, Paul kept urging all to take some food. He said, "Today is the fourteenth day that you have been waiting, going hungry and eating nothing. ³⁴I urge you, therefore, to take some food; it will help you survive. Not a hair of the head of anyone of you will be lost." ³⁵When he said this, he took bread, gave thanks to God in front of them all, broke it, and began to eat. ³⁶They were all encouraged, and took some food themselves. ³⁷In all, there were two hundred seventy-six of us on the ship. ³⁸After they had eaten enough, they lightened the ship by throwing the wheat into the sea.

³⁹When day came they did not recognize the land, but made out a bay with a beach. They planned to run the ship ashore on it, if they could. ⁴⁰So they cast off the anchors and abandoned them to the sea, and at the same time they unfastened the lines of the rudders, and hoisting the foresail into the wind, they made for the beach. ⁴¹But they struck a sandbar and ran the ship aground. The bow was wedged in and could not be moved, but the stern began to break up under the pounding [of the waves]. ⁴²The soldiers

continue

planned to kill the prisoners so that none might swim away and escape, [43]but the centurion wanted to save Paul and so kept them from carrying out their plan. He ordered those who could swim to jump overboard first and get to the shore, [44]and then the rest, some on planks, others on debris from the ship. In this way, all reached shore safely.

CHAPTER 28

Winter in Malta

[1]Once we had reached safety we learned that the island was called Malta. [2]The natives showed us extraordinary hospitality; they lit a fire and welcomed all of us because it had begun to rain and was cold. [3]Paul had gathered a bundle of brushwood and was putting it on the fire when a viper, escaping from the heat, fastened on his hand. [4]When the natives saw the snake hanging from his hand, they said to one another, "This man must certainly be a murderer; though he escaped the sea, Justice has not let him remain alive." [5]But he shook the snake off into the fire and suffered no harm. [6]They were expecting him to swell up or suddenly to fall down dead but, after waiting a long time and seeing nothing unusual happen to him, they changed their minds and began to say that he was a god. [7]In the vicinity of that place were lands belonging to a man named Publius, the chief of the island. He welcomed us and received us cordially as his guests for three days. [8]It so happened that the father of Publius was sick with a fever and dysentery. Paul visited him and, after praying, laid his hands on him and healed him. [9]After this had taken place, the rest of the sick on the island came to Paul and were cured. [10]They paid us great honor and when we eventually set sail they brought us the provisions we needed.

Arrival in Rome

[11]Three months later we set sail on a ship that had wintered at the island. It was an Alexandrian ship with the Dioscuri as its figurehead. [12]We put in at Syracuse and stayed there three days, [13]and

continue

material goods on the Christian journey of following Jesus, all the literally realistic details of dumping cargo, jettisoning gear, cutting off the dinghy, and abandoning anchors point to the need for traveling light to achieve salvation. (See Luke 10:4; 14:33; 18:25-27: " 'For it is easier for a camel to pass through the eye of a needle than for a rich person to enter the kingdom of God.' Those who heard this said, 'Then who can be saved?' And he said, 'What is impossible for human beings is possible for God.' ")

This is not to say that Luke has composed an allegory of Christian life in Acts 27. Rather, he has reported this tale of God's care of Paul and his mission in such a way that the historical account of nautical disaster and survival resonates with and alludes to the end-time situation of the church and the world. (We are "all in the same boat," and God is our only hope.) A further clue that Luke has this resonance in mind may be the fact that only his version of the synoptic tradition of the stilling of the storm pictures Jesus and the disciples as *sailing* (*pleontōn*, Luke 8:23).

28:1-10 Malta: hospitality, vindication, and healing

The story of the sea travel, including the "we" section that tells it, continues through the arrival in Rome (in verse 16, where the NABRE translates "he entered," the Greek has "*we* entered"). The safe arrival of all 276 on the shore of Malta leads to a supreme irony. Everything has been building, we readers have been led to believe, to a trial and judgment by the highest authority of the secular world, Caesar. But Luke will end his second volume without any mention of that Roman trial (which, tradition tells us, resulted in Paul's death). Instead, we are told of judgment by a lower, more spontaneous "court," reflecting the higher, divine judgment.

In Mediterranean antiquity, survival of disaster demonstrated divine favor. Luke calls the hospitable Maltese natives *barbaroi* (that is, non-Greek-speakers), but he speaks of their uncommon *philanthropia*. When they see Paul attacked by a snake, they interpret that as a

Malta in relation to Italy and Sicily

from there we sailed round the coast and arrived at Rhegium. After a day, a south wind came up and in two days we reached Puteoli. [14]There we found some brothers and were urged to stay with them for seven days. And thus we came to Rome. [15]The brothers from there heard about us and came as far as the Forum of Appius and Three Taverns to meet us. On seeing them, Paul gave thanks to God and took courage. [16]When he entered Rome, Paul was allowed to live by himself, with the soldier who was guarding him.

continue

sign of divine disfavor—indeed, proof that Paul is a murderer (v. 5). However, when he fails to swell up and drop dead, they call him a god! An overreaction, to be sure, but a powerful point has been made. As God had vindicated Jesus through resurrection, so he vindicates Paul through rescue from storm and snakebite. Further affirmation comes by way of Paul's ability to extend Jesus' healing ministry to the father of Governor Publius and other sick of the island who come to him.

28:11-31 Arrival in Rome and testimony to Jews

How a work ends is a matter of great importance to any careful author, especially in antiquity (recall Aristotle's stress on the importance of a beginning, middle, and end of a work). Luke chooses to end his two-volume work, not, as we already observed, with the expected Roman trial, but with several encounters between Paul and local Jewish leaders. Because these dialogues issue in "mixed reviews" at best and end with Paul quoting Isaiah 6:9-10 and turning once again to Gentiles,

some commentators have read this as a declaration that God has, at this point, severed his covenant relationship with the Jews. Since this kind of interpretation has supported Christian anti-Judaism, it is important to read Luke's narrative ending carefully, on its own terms.

The first contact that Paul and his two companions make on Italian soil is with people in Puteoli, whom Luke calls "brothers." Since it is the Gentile Luke who refers to them as brothers, the presumption is that they are fellow Christians. After a week of enjoying their hospitality (the Roman guard himself apparently glad for the break), they move on to the Forum of Appius and then to the rest stop called Three Taverns. At both places brothers come down from Rome to meet them. Paul's response to the brothers ("Paul gave thanks to God and took courage," v. 15) confirms the likelihood that these are also Christians. (The Christian community in Rome had been founded by others than Paul or Peter, possibly by the "travelers from Rome" [2:10] who had witnessed the birth of the church at Pentecost.)

The author James D. G. Dunn makes a charming interpretive conjecture regarding Luke's inclusion of the name of the Alexandrian ship that takes Paul's party to Rome, the *Dioscuri* ("Zeus's Boys," that is, Castor and Pollux, twin sons of the god Zeus). Noting that Luke uses "brothers" four times in the next few

---

Testimony to Jews in Rome

[17]Three days later he called together the leaders of the Jews. When they had gathered he said to them, "My brothers, although I had done nothing against our people or our ancestral customs, I was handed over to the Romans as a prisoner from Jerusalem. [18]After trying my case the Romans wanted to release me, because they found nothing against me deserving the death penalty. [19]But when the Jews objected, I was obliged to appeal to Caesar, even though I had no accusation to make against my own nation. [20]This is the reason, then, I have requested to see you and to speak with you, for it is on account of the hope of Israel that I wear these chains." [21]They answered him, "We have received no letters from Judea about you, nor has any of the brothers arrived with a damaging report or rumor about you. [22]But we should like to hear you present your views, for we know that this sect is denounced everywhere."

[23]So they arranged a day with him and came to his lodgings in great numbers. From early morning until evening, he expounded his position to them, bearing witness to the kingdom of God and trying to convince them about Jesus from the law of Moses and the prophets. [24]Some were convinced by what he had said, while others did not

continue

Caesarea have not found him guilty of anything warranting the death penalty, and his behavior is perfectly Jewish: he preaches "the hope of Israel." What is new is his hinting at the possibility (not pursued) of a countersuit (v. 19). They reply that they have heard nothing bad about him, by letter or hearsay. But they have heard about this controversial "sect" that he promotes, and they do want to learn more about that.

To this end, Paul holds an all-day conference with an even greater number of Jewish leaders, focusing on the heart of the matter: the kingdom of God and Jesus as fulfillment of the Scriptures. Some are convinced, others are not, and they leave without agreeing among themselves. As commentary on this divided response, Paul invokes Isaiah 6:9-10, implying that those who have failed to accept Jesus as the hope of Israel have fulfilled that prophecy. He adds, alluding to LXX Isa 40:5 (quoted earlier at Luke 3:6), that "this salvation of God has been sent to the Gentiles; they will listen."

Does this final word of Paul mean that the door is closed to further mission to Israel? No more than the presence of Isaiah 6:9-10 in the original commission of Isaiah of Jerusalem indicated that he had no mission to his people (belied by the sixty chapters that follow in the scroll of Isaiah). The rejection of the gospel by the majority of historical Israel is, for Luke, a fact to be faced. But this fact, and the turn to the Gentiles, is no more a definitive dismissal of the Jews than are the parallel moments in the synagogues of Pisidian Antioch (13:46-47) or Corinth (18:6). In ending with this episode, Luke has helped his (largely Gentile) readers understand (a) their relationship to historical Israel, (b) the majority of Israel's rejection of its Messiah, and (c) how the Gentiles have become beneficiaries of Israel's vocation to be a "light to the nations" (Isa 49:6).

Meanwhile, in the spirit of the parables of the barren fig tree (Luke 13:6-9) and two lost sons (Luke 15:11-32), the door remains open. In Paul's continued ministry during his house arrest, he receives "*all* who came to him" (emphasis added). He models the community's

verses, first of Christians then of Jews, this author suggests that Luke calls attention to the name of the ship because for him the Christian and Jewish "brothers" that Paul is about to encounter are "indeed twin children of the one God, brothers of Paul, and so of one another."

Once established in Rome, apparently under house arrest in his own rented lodgings (v. 28), Paul calls together (non-Christian) Jewish leaders, who are also called "brothers" (vv. 17 and 21). His purpose is a kind of preemptive defense. Since the plaintiffs in his case are the Jerusalem Jews, he presents his apologia to their Roman counterparts. For us readers, the defense is familiar: the Roman authorities in ongoing mission as "he proclaimed the kingdom of God and taught about the Lord Jesus Christ with boldness of speech [*meta parrēsias*], without hindrance [*akōlytōs*]" (v. 31, my translation). Note that the last two words powerfully affirm the theme of freedom running through the whole of Acts; *parrēsia* is that same freedom and boldness of speech for which the community prayed in Acts 4:29 and which the leaders exhibit throughout Acts (2:29; 4:13, 31; 9:27-28; 13:46; 14:3; 18:26; 19:8; and 26:25). And the final word, *akōlytōs* ("without hindrance") reminds us that neither the one who was sent to proclaim release to prisoners (Luke 4:18) nor his Spirit-led followers were hindered by imprisonment or even death.

Luke's two-volume work, which began in the Jerusalem temple, ends with the mission continuing unabated in a rented Roman apartment. In the end, Luke's history is not so much about Peter or Paul as about the fidelity of God and the continuing prophetic mission of the followers of Jesus. If the ending of Acts surprises us by failing to include the martyrdom of Paul (which was surely known to Luke), that very inconclusiveness serves to remind us that we are invited to continue the story with our lives.

believe. [25]Without reaching any agreement among themselves they began to leave; then Paul made one final statement. "Well did the holy Spirit speak to your ancestors through the prophet Isaiah, saying:

[26]'Go to this people and say:
You shall indeed hear but not understand.
    You shall indeed look but never see.
[27]Gross is the heart of this people;
    they will not hear with their ears;
        they have closed their eyes,
so they may not see with their eyes
    and hear with their ears
and understand with their heart and be
        converted,
    and I heal them.'

[28]Let it be known to you that this salvation of God has been sent to the Gentiles; they will listen." [[29]]

[30]He remained for two full years in his lodgings. He received all who came to him, [31]and with complete assurance and without hindrance he proclaimed the kingdom of God and taught about the Lord Jesus Christ.

Ruins of the Roman Forum

EXPLORING LESSON FOUR

1. Chapters 25 and 26 of Acts describe a kind of merry-go-round of charges, hearings, and defenses involving Paul and various Jewish and Roman leaders. What explains all the jostling of characters? What seems to be happening?

_____

_____

_____

_____

_____

2. What strikes you about Paul's answer to the charges brought against him in Caesarea (25:10-11)? Do you know of others throughout history who have faced persecution because of their faith and sought to defend themselves with the truth?

_____

_____

_____

_____

_____

3. In the three accounts of Paul's encounter with the risen Lord on the way to Damascus, light and blindness play an important role. In this final description, how have these two elements shifted to highlight another facet of the experience (26:12-18)?

_____

_____

_____

_____

_____

4. What is the irony in Paul's appeal to Caesar (26:30-32)? How does God use this for a divine purpose?

_____

_____

_____

_____

_____

_____

5. The centurion escorting Paul to Rome ignores Paul's warning about a shipwreck, no doubt because the warning came from a prisoner (27:9-20). How can we help assure our own openness to hearing what God might be saying to us from unlikely sources? (See 1 Thess 5:21.)

_____

_____

_____

_____

_____

6. Identify the eucharistic actions and undertones in the account of Paul sharing a meal with those on the ship (27:34-38). (See Luke 9:16; 22:19; 24:30; Matt 14:19; 15:36.)

_____

_____

_____

_____

_____

7. a) Who are the first people Paul meets with in Rome (28:17)?

_____

_____

_____

_____

   b) How does Paul convince them of Jesus' identity (28:23)?

_____

_____

_____

_____

8. a) The Acts of the Apostles ends in a way that seems a bit unfinished: no trial or martyrdom of Paul, no more information about the church community in Rome, etc. Why do you think Luke may have ended his story this way?

_____

_____

_____

_____

b) This unusual ending to a momentous story serves as a reminder that the work of God's people is unfinished. How do you understand this work? What is left to do? (See Luke 24:48-49; John 14:12-14; 20:21-22; 1 Cor 12:27-31.)

_____

_____

_____

_____

_____

9. Several times in the accounts of the early church in Acts, the Holy Spirit makes important interventions to guide the community (e.g., 8:26-39; 10:24-48; 16:7). In your lifetime, what are some of the most significant interventions of the Holy Spirit in the life of the church?

_____

_____

_____

_____

_____

10. Reflect back on your study of the Acts of the Apostles. What was your favorite story, or what did you find most meaningful? What will you take with you as you look to the future of our contemporary church?

_____

_____

_____

_____

_____

_____

_____

CLOSING PRAYER

Prayer

*. . . [Paul] proclaimed the kingdom of God
and taught about the Lord Jesus
Christ.* (Acts 28:31)

We pray in the words of St. Teresa of Avila:

Christ has no body now but yours. No hands, no feet
    on earth but yours.
Yours are the eyes through which he looks compas-
    sion on this world.
Yours are the feet with which he walks to do good.
Yours are the hands through which he blesses all
    the world.
Yours are the hands, yours are the feet, yours are the
    eyes, you are his body.
Christ has no body now on earth but yours.

God of the good news, we pray for the joy of the gospel
and the strength of its earliest messengers. Make us
effective ministers of your word so that those we meet
will recognize your son in each of us. We pray for the
ministries where we serve, and the ministries we hope to
do, as together we continue the story of your church . . .

PRAYING WITH YOUR GROUP

Because we know that the Bible allows us to hear God's voice, prayer provides the context for our study and sharing. By speaking and listening to God and each other, the discussion often grows to more deeply bond us to one another and to God.

At *the beginning and end of each lesson* simple prayers are provided for individual use, and also may be used within the group setting. Most of the closing prayers provided with each lesson relate directly to a theme from that lesson and encourage you to pray together for people and events in your local community.

Of course, there are many ways to center ourselves in God's presence as we gather together in groups around the word of God. We provide some additional suggestions here knowing you and your group will make prayer a priority as part of your gathering. These are simply alternative ways to pray if your group would like to try something different from those prayers provided in the previous pages.

Conversational Prayer

This form of prayer allows for the group members to pray in their own words in a way that is not intimidating. The group leader begins with Step One, inviting all to focus on the presence of Christ among them. After a few moments of quiet, the group leader invites anyone in the group to voice a prayer or two of thanksgiving; once that is complete, then anyone who has personal intentions may pray in their own words for their needs; finally, the group prays for the needs of others.

A suggested process:
In your own words, speak simple and short prayers to allow time for others to add their voices.

Focus on one "step" at a time, not worrying about praying for everything in your mental list at once.

Step One	Visualize Christ. Welcome him. Imagine him present with you in your group. Allow time for some silence.
Step Two	Gratitude opens our hearts. Use simple words such as, "Thank you, Lord, for . . ."
Step Three	Pray for your own needs knowing that others will pray with you. Be specific and honest. Use "I" and "me" language.

| Step Four | Pray for others by name, with love.
You may voice your agreement ("Yes, Lord").
End with gratitude for sharing concerns. |

Praying Like Ignatius

St. Ignatius Loyola, whose life and ministry are the foundation of the Jesuit community, invites us to enter into Scripture texts in order to experience the scenes, especially scenes of the gospels or other narrative parts of Scripture. Simply put, this is a method of creatively imagining the scene, viewing it from the inside, and asking God to meet you there. Most often, this is a personal form of prayer, but in a group setting, some of its elements can be helpful if you allow time for this process.

A suggested process:

- Select a scene from the chapters in the particular lesson.
- Read that scene out loud in the group, followed by some quiet time.
- Ask group members to place themselves in the scene (as a character, or as an onlooker) so that they can imagine the emotions, responses, and thinking that may have taken place. Notice the details and the tone, and imagine the interaction with the Lord that is taking place.
- Share with the group any insights that came to you in this quiet imagining.
- Allow each person in the group to thank God for some insight and to pray about some request that may have surfaced.

Sacred Reading (or Lectio Divina)

This method of prayer invites us to "listen with the ear of the heart" as St. Benedict's rule would say. We listen to the words and the phrasing, asking God to speak to our innermost being. Again, this method of prayer is most often used in an individual setting but may also be used in an adapted way within a group.

A suggested process:

- Select a scene from the chapters in the particular lesson.
- Read the scene out loud in the group, perhaps two times.
- Ask group members to ponder a word or phrase that stands out to them.
- The group members could then simply speak the word or phrase as a kind of litany of what was meaningful for your group.
- Allow time for more silence to ponder the words that were heard, asking God to reveal to you what message you are meant to hear, how God is speaking to you.
- Follow up with spoken intentions at the close of this group time.

REFLECTING ON SCRIPTURE

Reading Scripture is an opportunity not simply to learn new information but to listen to God who loves you. Pray that the same Holy Spirit who guided the formation of Scripture will inspire you to correctly understand what you read, and empower you to make what you read a part of your life.

The inspired word of God contains layers of meaning. As you make your way through passages of Scripture, whether studying a book of the Bible or focusing on a biblical theme, you may find it helpful to ask yourself these four questions:

What does the Scripture passage say?
Read the passage slowly and reflectively. Become familiar with it. If the passage you are reading is a narrative, carefully observe the characters and the plot. Use your imagination to picture the scene or enter into it.

What does the Scripture passage mean?
Read the footnotes in your Bible and the commentary provided to help you understand what the sacred writers intended and what God wants to communicate by means of their words.

What does the Scripture passage mean to me?
Meditate on the passage. God's word is living and powerful. What is God saying to you? How does the Scripture passage apply to your life today?

What am I going to do about it?
Try to discover how God may be challenging you in this passage. An encounter with God contains a challenge to know God's will and follow it more closely in daily life. Ask the Holy Spirit to inspire not only your mind but your life with this living word.